Published by Periplus Editions
with editorial offices at
130 Joo Seng Road #06-01
Singapore 368357

Copyright © 2002 Periplus Editions (HK) Ltd.

ISBN: 962-593-991-1

Library of Congress
Control Number: 2002101481

Photo credits
All food and location photography by Jean-François Hamon.
Additional photos by Luca Invernizzi Tettoni (page 2).

Endpaper: Painting by M. Spiewak Misia.

Distributed by

USA
Tuttle Publishing
364 Innovation Drive
North Clarendon, VT 05759-9436
USA
Tel: (802) 773-8930
Fax: (802) 773-6993

Japan and Korea
Tuttle Publishing
RK Building 2nd Floor
2-13-10 Shimo-Meguro, Meguro-Ku
Tokyo 153 0064, Japan
Tel: (81-3) 5437-0171
Fax: (81-3) 5437-0755

Asia Pacific
Berkeley Books Pte. Ltd.
130 Joo Seng Road #06-01
Singapore 368357
Tel: (65) 6280-1330
Fax: (65) 6280-6290

First Edition
Printed in Singapore

THE FOOD OF
PARIS

Authentic Recipes from Parisian Bistros and Restaurants

by Marie-Noël Rio
Photography by Jean-François Hamon
Styling by Sophie Jacquesson
Translation by Vincent Vichit-Vadakan

Feauturing recipes from the following restaurants:

A & M Le Bistrot   Paris Main d'Or
Chez Casimir   Rôtisserie du Beaujolais
Chez Catherine   Saint-Antoine
Marty   Le Train Bleu
Mollard   Le Troquet
Les Olivades   Le Zéphyr

PERIPLUS

Contents

Part One: Food in Paris

A slice of culinary history

The identity of France—the European nation with the longest history of tenacious centralized government—and the identity of Paris, its capital, have been closely intertwined for centuries. Since the 13th century, when Philippe-Auguste built the fortifications around the city and set up his royal palace, Paris has been the stage on which French social mores have always been defined. And none more so than the tradition of food, which has played a major role in French society since the Middle Ages.

In Medieval times the subtleties of fine dining were only enjoyed by the ruling classes. The poor contented themselves day in day out with a diet of black bread and gruel. The kitchens of the Court served white bread with tender meat of poultry and game, spices, and exotic fruits, washed down with generous amounts of claret or other headier wines. Dairy products, most red meat, and vegetables were left to the commoners, along with cheap wines, cider, and beer.

In the 17th century, the heart of France was neither Paris nor Versailles, but the body of Louis XIV, the Sun King. When his power was at its zenith, the King's meals—like the rest of his private life—were lavish affairs attended by the notables of the day. Cooking took a decisive turn. La Quintinie, who benefited from being in the King's favor, made orchards and vegetable-growing fashionable; the use of spices was abandoned, and the star chefs of the day stigmatized "the old-fashioned and disgusting manner of preparing things" as being "gothic" cuisine. Food became an affair of state, in fact to such an extent that Vatel, who was responsible for the King's entertainment and his table during a visit to the Prince de Condé, chose suicide when his delivery of fish failed to materialize on time. Of course, such considerations only concerned nobility. Commoners for their part were starved as never before.

In the 18th century, the Regent took up quarters in Paris, far from the outdated etiquette

Page 2:
The Champs-Elysées is one of the most fashionable streets in Paris and is lined with numerous cafés and restaurants.

Opposite:
Opposite St. Lazare train station, the Brasserie Mollard is an Art Nouveau masterpiece. In the foreground, Scallops with Citrus Vinaigrette (see recipe on page 64).

Left:
An intimate aristocratic supper in the 18th century.

A typical scene in a bourgeois restaurant from days gone by, with the ceremonial carving of a calf's head, served with traditional sauce ravigote.

Gourmands, formed a jury of tasters and invented the food review. A little later, Jean-Anthelme Brillat-Savarin's *Physiology of Taste* raised a veritable temple to the art of gastronomy. Both works placed culinary art and all that goes with it (wines, the order of serving dishes, table settings, conversations, table etiquette) at the center of French culture, and made Paris the arbiter of taste, in both senses of the word, in flavors and esthetics. La Reynière, in his *Ecrits Gastronomiques*, described the paradox thus: "Though Paris itself produces nothing, for not a grain of wheat grows there, not a single lamb is born there, not one cauliflower is harvested there, it is the center where everything from every corner of the globe lands, because it is the place where the respective qualities of all that man uses as food is most appreciated, and where such things are best transformed for our sensual pleasure." Brillat-Savarin declared: "Animals feed themselves; man eats; but only the wise man knows how to eat."

Today, cooking interests all people at every level of society. The poor may not eat like the rich, but the passion for food crosses the barriers of social class and everyone, aprt from those who eat only to survive, can develop the knowledge of food that results in real pleasure.

Paris today, like Paris in the 19th century, is unanimously a city of food lovers. Talk about food with a Parisian, in the street, at the bar of a café, or on a bus, and his eyes will light up, his attitude will soften, and his warmth will shine through. He could go on forever. He, for one, knows how to eat.

of Versailles. Pleasure, once rejected by Madame de Maintenon because of her fear of eternal damnation, came back into fashion. The first restaurants appeared and caused a furor, making antiquated taverns and inns unstylish, too rugged for civilized tastes. The French Revolution brought an end to aristocratic privilege and introduced a relative democratization of manners. Alexandre Grimod de la Reynière, author of the *Almanach des*

A Job for Connoisseurs

Preserving traditions and promoting innovation

Ever since the 14th century, French cuisine has been rigorously codified. *Le Viandier* (an anonymous work erroneously attributed to Taillevent, Head of the Royal Kitchens under Charles VI) and *Le Ménagier de Paris* (compiled from existing cookery books by an elderly Parisian bourgeois who aimed to teach his young wife the virtues of economy as well as cooking) were hugely successful and served as the benchmark for works up to the beginning of the 17th century.

Le Cuisinier Français by La Varenne, published in 1651, marked the birth of French *haute cuisine*. Ever since then, from Antonin Carême to Auguste Escoffier, from Curnonsky to Ginette Mathiot, the complex history of culinary techniques, fashions, and tastes has been woven by numerous authors, chefs, gourmets, critics, and housewives. Hardly a day passes it seems without a cookbook being published, or a chef writing his own.

All of this literature extends far beyond the daily requirements of most people, often into the realms of fiction. In the past, recipes included few if no details concerning quantities and preparation and cooking times, as can be seen in the recipe for Mock Sturgeon made from Veal. Today's cookbooks are not always more practical for the novice, either due to lack of experience—the best chefs are not necessarily the best teachers—or lack of time. Still, the vast array of culinary works that have been published have contributed greatly, just as much as the actual cooking and eating, to the aura of refinement that surrounds French cuisine.

ESTURGEON CONTREFAIT DE VEAU
(Mock Sturgeon made from Veal)

For six servings. either the night before or early in the morning, take six calves' heads, without skinning them. Scald them in warm water, as you would a pig, and then cook them in wine; add a mug of vinegar, salt and boil them until overripe meat falls from the bones. Then leave the heads to cool before boning. Then take a large piece of rough canvas, wrap it tightly round the heads, sew it up like a square pillow, place it between two planks and set a very heavy weight on top. Leave it standing like this all night. Cut into slices, removing the skin, as with venison, season with parsley and vinegar. Only two slices per serving.

Le Ménagier de Paris, circa 1393

In Paris, the City of Lights, dining out is a must. In the 16th century, the courtiers of Henri III were already patronizing the Tour d'Argent, and Henri VI was most partial to their heron pâté. This reputed hostelry, established in 1582, has since become a restaurant—one of the most famous in the world—and has moved from the ground floor up to the sixth. It is a shining example of the continuity of Parisian traditions.

The term "restaurant," which used to refer to a fortifying meat broth and, by analogy, the establishments which served it to their clients, acquired its modern meaning in 1765 when a certain Monsieur Boulanger proposed individual

---

RECIPE FOR A « RESTAURANT » OR RESTORATIVE MEAT BROTH

The restaurant is made from beef, mutton, veal, capon, young pigeon, partridge, onions, root vegetables and fine herbs. It is steamed, but without using any liquid, in a pot whose lid is sealed with pastry. The pot is put in a bain-marie for five to six hours, after which this decidedly succulent broth is sieved and the fat removed. Once this operation has been completed, then a loaf of bread is hollowed out and is filled with the minced and seasoned meat from capons and other fine cuts, before being poached in the bubbling broth. Before serving, it is garnished with cockscombs, calf sweetbread and other delicacies browned in smoked bacon.

---

tables to his diners at his establishment on the rue du Louvre, as well as an extensive choice of dishes at fixed prices (including the famous broth). It was an outstanding success. In 1782, Antoine Beauvilliers, former chef to the Count of Provence (the future Louis XVIII) opened his Grande Taverne de Londres on rue de Richelieu, aimed at a refined clientele, following a model that had become highly popular in England. The whole of Paris society flocked to it and the establishment did not finally close its doors until 1925. At the time of the Revolution, Paris boasted less than 100 restaurants; a few years later there were more than 500, of which several still exist today. Their arrival proved to be the knockout blow for the various guilds that had formed during the Middle Ages (for example, caterers lost the privilege of being the sole vendors of cooked meat), while chefs of the various aristocrats who had fled into exile now switched their talents to altogether different customers. Public life experienced unprecedented growth. The two centuries that followed more than confirmed Monsieur Boulanger's intuition, and Paris now boasts some 10,000 establishments (though not all can be recommended, alas!). Although chefs, styles, and neighborhoods can be built up and then sent crashing down by the vagaries of fashion, restaurants remain essential and firmly embedded parts of Parisian culture and tradition, with the best houses enjoying remarkable longevity.

Today, the great restaurants are the heirs of sophisticated and costly aristocratic culinary traditions (one of the most reputed establishments

Chartier, on the rue du Faubourg-Montmartre is one of the few surviving examples of the celebrated bouillons in Paris. Opened in 1896, it has been declared a historical monument.

Le Train Bleu, the station restaurant at the Gare de Lyon, was inaugurated by the French president in 1901. It is the most striking example of the Belle Epoque style in France.

photocopied or chalked-up on blackboards are reminders of the old *bouillons* where bank clerks, administrative pen-pushers and shop assistants would have regaled themselves a century ago with good homely fare at modest prices. Whatever social castes they cater to, they have their regulars and nothing is more pleasing to a Parisian's vanity than being recognized, greeted by name and treated with respect wherever he may choose to eat, regardless his wealth or social status. Prick up your ears in a Parisian eatery and you will hear nothing but praise, criticisms, and opinions concerning the food and drink, for in Paris there is no pleasure without comment.

To complete the picture, it is important to add that the Louis XIV complex, which is still virulent, and the attachment to the "greatness" of France, nay the certitude of her superiority, do little to encourage a more open approach on the part of the French towards other culinary styles. Cuisine from all over the world can be found in Paris, with any exotic whim catered to, not to mention the gradual integration of certain "foreign" ingredients (such as Parmesan and Balsamic vinegar), but do they consider it to be "real" cuisine? It is true however that this French ethnocentrism, while doing little to improve a nation's command of foreign languages or its respect of basic rules of hospitality, serves our purposes to perfection.

Every great culinary tradition, as well as being a breeding ground of inventiveness and experimentation is first and foremost a keeper of traditional tastes and practices.

of Paris employs a team of 48 people for 45 covers). Smart restaurants and trendy bistros evoke the establishments of the 18th and 19th centuries as depicted in art and literature. The brasseries that grew and prospered in the 19th century have seen a renewal of interest over the last few years, due to their traditional bourgeois cuisine and flamboyant decor. The more earthy bistros with their *plats du jour* (daily specials) and their menus

Paris and the Provinces

*The cuisine of the capital city represents
a convergence of all French provincial culinary talent*

Only two of the fourteen chefs who contributed recipes to this book were born in Paris and even they are first-generation Parisians: one has parents from the regions of Charentes and Brittany on the Atlantic coast, while the other's parents originally came from Normandy and the Périgord. The others together represent nine different French provinces and their distinct cuisines, plus one chef from Japan whose cooking shows a distinct enthusiasm for the food from the Basque country. The siren song of the capital has long attracted the ambitious: how can you keep them "down on the farm" when they dream of making a name for themselves and revealing their talent to the world? When chefs come to Paris seeking fame or fortune, their bags are packed with local products and local savoir-faire. So even the most Parisian of dishes are provincial in origin: fresh seafood comes from Brittany and Normandy, *escargots* from Burgundy, *salade niçoise* from Nice, warm lentil salad and andouillette sausage from Lyon,

potatoes *au gratin* from the Dauphiné, *choucroute* from Alsace. It is true that the flavors of the provinces are adapted to suit the Parisian table, and in the process gain something spiritual, subtle, and elegant, even down to the humblest dish of offal. Cooking in Paris allows the chef artistic license that would not be granted elsewhere. Parisians meanwhile are absolutely passionate about the authenticity of regional traditions and celebrate peasant dishes, handmade charcuterie, and the desserts their grandmothers served. This is even more pronounced because it comes on the heels of the oh-so-precious nouvelle cuisine. It also explains their refusal to submit to fast-food and other forms of culinary globalization—feasting on a heritage handed down by generations of connoisseurs is one way of keeping the taste buds from being dulled. Drinking is another: Parisian wine bars are temples to the glory of Burgundy, Touraine or Bordeaux and the arrival of *beaujolais nouveau* every autumn is a much awaited event.

Le Rallye du Nord, like thousands of Paris bistros, announces the day's specials directly on its windows. Inside, dishes are listed on blackboards.

Seasonal Cuisine

Authenticity and precision, the keys to perfection

Curnonsky, prince of gourmets, declared that: "Cuisine is when things taste like what they are." This astonishing paradox is probably the best definition of French cooking, where the highest art consists of doing away with the most erudite techniques to serve a dish that blends textures, tastes, and cooking methods to produce something that appears as nature intended.

Good cuisine starts at the market, where every product has its high season. Everyone knows that you cannot find wild mushrooms or game out of season, but few people realize that all meat and seafood also have their moments of perfection, which vary from species to species, just like fruit and vegetables. Whether you are seeking higher quality or better prices, there are many advantages in buying products at the height of their season.

It is thus important to be able to evaluate the freshness of a piece of fish, the quality of a cut of meat, and the ripeness of a vegetable or fruit, as well as the happy (or unhappy) marriages between various ingredients. A novice would be wise to follow the advice of a good recipe, a friendly cook or a competent grocer: nothing delights honest craftsmen or enlightened people more than sharing their experience and knowledge with anyone who is truly eager to learn. In general, specialist grocers, experts in what they sell, are preferable to supermarkets where you have to sort the best from the worst, and where it is hard to get away from industrial production.

Finally, it is better to make your purchases as near to mealtime as possible, to avoid having to stock them in the refrigerator, which is always bad for fresh ingredients. This may seem rather complicated, but with a successful trip to the market you will already have taken a big step towards culinary triumph.

The menus of good Parisian restaurants change at least once a season and have a different market dish or menu every day, often composed that very

the oven and the flesh will be unpleasantly tough. Over-boil baby vegetables and they will be irremediably ruined, becoming soft and tasteless. On the other hand, if you do not give the meat for a stew the hours of cooking it requires in order to reach the desired tenderness, it will be inedible.

Cooking techniques (grilling, frying, roasting, braising, steaming, boiling, simmering) are simple but precise, and require a little organization and the right equipment (see page 29). Sauces have become considerably lighter. But that does not mean that cream, butter and classical beurre blanc have been banished from the Parisian kitchen, where they are still used with moderation to enrich cooking juices and coulis. Variations are infinite, although the basic techniques are in fact few in number. The thick sauces made with a flour roux, once a mainstay of any decent French kitchen, have all but disappeared.

Now, more than ever before, Parisian cuisine concentrates on freshness, quality of products, and precise execution, which is hardly compatible with industrial agriculture. Today's high-technology agiculture produces tomatoes all year round in a nutritive liquid under neon lights, perfect in appearance and perfectly insipid in taste, and provides unbelievably red mid-winter strawberries that have the taste and consistency of papier mâché.

If you are in a hurry why not prepare one of those many very simple Parisian dishes that are tasty and quick to make? Not only will you increase your dining pleasure but you'll do no harm to your health either.

morning according to what delights they have gleaned from their purveyors' stalls.

Once the preparation itself begins in earnest, success depends above all on precision in cooking. Overcook a sea-bream by just a few minutes and its delicate flesh will turn to mush, whereas doing the same to an oily fish will give it more or less the appearance and consistency of an old shoe. Forget to let a duck rest after removing it from

The Belly of Paris

Eight centuries of fresh produce
in the heart of the capital

All Paris markets, grocers, and restaurants that have any pretensions to quality, stock up between 2 am and noon from Monday to Saturday, at the wholesale food market of Rungis.

This 232 hectare behemoth (larger than the Principality of Monaco), located 5 miles south of the capital, handles 2,000,000 tons of food produce a year and feeds 18,000,000 people. It is the biggest fresh-produce market in the world. The goods, which are counted in crates, trays, pallets, trolleys, and transport containers are reserved for those in the food trade.

Les Halles, circa 1930. The bustle in front of one of Baltard's pavilions at dawn.

Rungis Market opened on March 3, 1969. It took just forty-eight hours and a fleet of trucks to move what had been the Paris market since the start of the 12th century, the famous Halles that had had its praises sung by countless writers and poets. It has been said that the rats which flooded *Le ventre de Paris*, The Belly of Paris, as Emile Zola entitled one of his novels, followed the great move, but that is perhaps just malicious conjecture.

King Louis VI, the Fat (!), established the public Champeaux Market in 1136, on the site which the Halles occupied until their demise. The Guild of Halles Strongmen appeared during the reign of Saint Louis. Aragon describes them in his own poetic manner in Les Beaux Quartiers: "Sluggish yet nimble men with their bare, muscular arms, they seemed to be milking the formidable teats of a nurturing night." By the time of the move to Rungis, these Strongmen were still expected to be capable of carrying loads weighing 400 lb (200 kg) a distance of 60 meters!

During the 16th century François I ordered the reformation of the Halles and by the time of the French Revolution, it would specialize only in foodstuffs. Napoleon III was responsible for contracting Victor Baltard to design the warehouses which were constructed between 1854 and 1868 (the last two of which were only completed in 1936), giving the market its appearance that was familiar to Parisians until it closed in 1969.

In this gargantuan whole-sale market, you could find the rarest, freshest, finest products, from the best sources. This tradition of quality dates back to the Middle Ages with its litany of "shad from Bordeaux, sturgeon from Blaye, conger eels from La Rochelle, lampreys from Nantes, cuttle-fish from Coutances, herring from Fécamp, loach from Bar-sur-Seine, salmon from the Loire, pimperneaux eels from the Eure, barbel from Saint-Florentin, crayfish from Bar, pike from Châlons, trout from Andéli, dace from Aise, pâté from Paris, tarts from Dourlens, flans from Chartres, beer from Cambrai, tripe from Saint-Denis, cheese from Brie, chestnuts from Lombardy, purée from Arras, mustard from Dijon, pears from Saint-Rieule, garlic from Gandeluz, onions from Corbeil, shallots from Etampes." To this list, of which several entries still exist, today we could add butter from Echiré, potatoes from the Ile de Ré, prunes from Agen, Salers beef, lamb from Sisteron, Lyon sausage, walnuts from Grenoble, goose *foie gras* from Alsace, duck *foie gras* from the Landes, ceps from the Périgord, Guérande sea salt, duck from Challans, chicken from Loué, goose

The fresh fish market at Rungis. At three in the morning, when activity is in full swing.

from Touraine, Bayonne ham, jam from Bar-le-Duc, and olives from Nice, among many others. The market also sells products from around the globe, including some of the most exquisite and beautiful exotic fruits.

With the disappearance of Les Halles as a market, the night life of Paris changed. The restaurant Le Pied de Cochon is still open twenty-four hours a day, but you no longer see, clustered round the bar in the early hours, the night workers bolstering themselves with an umpteenth, dirt-cheap coffee or a snack washed down with a glass of Côtes-du-Rhône, while the merrymakers on the first-floor pay dearly for their peasant fare of pork trotters and frites or French onion soup. All that transits today through this now renovated quarter are tourists, both foreign and local, seeking the spirit of Les Halles, but without the tumult, smells, lights, bustle, and mountains of produce that characterized the old Halles.

Despite turning the page on such a long history, there is some consolation in noting that Paris still overflows with memories and signs of the past on virtually every street. The existing markets scattered all over the capital are just one example of this, whether they be covered, like the Secrétan, Saint-Quentin or Saint-Honoré markets, the busy shopping neighborhoods on the rue des Martyrs, rue Daguerre or rue Mouffetard, or the roaming markets, whose stalls fill the streets 2 or 3 days a week, like the rue de Convention, avenue de Saxe, avenue de Neuilly, or boulevard Barbès. Unfortunately some markets, like the one in the rue de Buci, have kept their traditional appearance (open stalls and barrows) but sell the industrial produce of the supermarkets that have bought their businesses. There are some stalls here and there selling produce of truly mediocre quality, but fortunately most of the tradespeople are excellent purveyors, proud of their trade and their knowledge, jealously maintaining a secular tradition of freshness and quality. That is where the Parisian will find that night's delivery of fresh fish, perfect meat and charcuterie, fruit and vegetables from open fields, cream that is truly the *crème de la crème*, mature cheese and, often, goods imported directly from their own countries by the Portuguese, Spanish and Italians who have long been an integral part of the life of the capital.

Finally, all of the Paris neighborhoods boast honest and competent merchants whose shops are never empty, whether they offer fresh produce like the market, or goods like bread, confectionery, cakes, cured meats or freshly prepared meals.

Les Halles may have gone and the slaughter-houses closed (both the horsemeat slaughter-houses of Vaugirard and the enormous abattoirs of La Villette) but Paris is still a world capital of fine cuisine. That people still wish to learn about it, cook it or taste it, as well as being demanding both at the market and in restaurants, is the surest sign that this status will remain for years to come.

Bread, Cheese, and Wine

The holy trinity of French gastronomy

Once the basis of the French diet, bread—or rather breads of innumerable description— is now a mere accompaniment to food. But what an accompaniment it is! Only shops where bread is kneaded and baked on the premises may be called *boulangeries*, or bakeries. Parisian bakers who had at one point succumbed to the siren song of cheap, quick, industrial products, have now largely gone back to quality ingredients and traditional techniques, including sourdough, long kneading times, and baking in wood ovens.

Good bread is dense, rather heavy, and has an unmistakable smell of flour with just a zest of acidity. After years of mediocrity, the *baguette*, a veritable symbol of France along with camembert and the beret, and probably the most famous form of bread in the world, has once again become the object of jealously guarded attentions. Whatever the secrets of its production, a good *baguette* must have a crisp, golden crust, a dense crumb with irregular air holes that is creamy white, almost ivory in color.

Besides the *flûte* (a thinner and shorter loaf) and the *baguette*, other popular breads include the *boule de campagne au levain* or sourdough loaf; the *fougasse provençale*, a dense, tressed bread made plain or with olives; organic whole wheat breads; rye bread with or without raisins; walnut or hazelnut breads often made from a blend of rye and wheat, and many other baked specialties. The art of choosing which type of bread to offer depends on the food served: toasted country loaves with *foie gras*; rye with oysters; walnut, hazelnut or raisin bread with a cheese platter. But simplest of pleasures in Paris is the *baguette*, hot from the oven, the crust crisp and the white inside soft and melting, eaten plain or spread with fresh butter.

Cheese is another example of extraordinary French *savoir-faire*. Curnonsky, between the world wars, catalogued 483 types of French cheese. By the 1960s, there were only 289. Today, with those that have resisted industrial normalization (some 200 cow's, ewe's or goat's milk cheeses),

A cheese shop worthy of the name will offer a large range of perfectly ripe cheeses.

ripe. It is not a job for the faint-hearted. Some fragile cheeses have a delicate maturing process, followed by a few fleeting days of perfection and then rapid deterioration. Without any preservatives, a fresh set cheese can quickly turn sour. A scrupulous shopkeeper will discard any product that is past its prime. His reputation, the foundation of continued prosperity, will gain from what he might lose in his short-term profits.

The most famous cow's milk cheeses are the soft cheeses with a mild rind like the coulommiers from the Ile-de-France region outside Paris, brie from Meaux or camembert from Normandy. There are cured soft cheeses, often in brine, like Pont l'évêque and Livarot from Nor-

France is still the unchallenged leader in the field.

We will not discuss pasteurized cheeses here, those mass-produced dairy products sold in refrigerator cases (the surest way of destroying any semblance of taste), but of farmhouse cheeses that generations of craftsmen have made sublime. In Paris they are sold by merchants who have a real love of their profession, who age them in their cellars and sell them only in season and only when

mandy or Maroilles, that was documented in the 12th century and the heart-shaped Rollot that Louis XIV loved (both from northern France). There are pressed, uncooked cheeses like Reblochon from the Alps, Saint-nectaire (best in summer and autumn) and Cantal, both from central France and described in Diderot's encyclopedia. And finally there are the pressed cooked varieties, including the famous Alpine Gruyère, and Comté and Beaufort, from the region of Franche-Comté.

The Vacherin-mont-d'or from the Jura is eaten with a spoon and is available in the winter months only. Epoisses is aged with *marc*, spirits of Burgundy wine. Pungent Munster from Alsace is given more character with cumin seeds. Saint-marcellin from the Dauphiné melts onto its straw mat, and was much to the taste of Louis XI.

Don't overlook the delicacy of *fromage frais*, fresh cheese, curdled and drained, that is served as a dessert either plain, with salt and pepper, sweetened with sugar or with fruit sauces or compotes. Pick a *fromage frais* that is not industrial, made from whole milk and has not had air whipped into it. Faisselle from the Lyon region, topped with fresh cream, are a little taste of heaven.

Blue cheeses, cultivated with penicillium, are made from cow's milk, like the Fourme d'Ambert, or the blues from Auvergne, Causses or Gex, or from ewe's milk, like the most famous blue, the Roquefort, that Casanova claimed to be an aphrodisiac in his memoirs.

Ewe's milk cheese are generally found in the Béarn like Esbareich, in Basque country like Ardigasna or in Corsica like Venaco. In Provence, there is a fresh curdled cheese, the Brousse de Rove, a cousin of Corsican Broccio.

Goat's cheeses form a large family: Cabecou from Gascony, Crottin de Chavignol, Loire Valley Sainte-maure, Valençay, Pouligny-saint-pierre, Brique de Forez, Pélardon from the Cévennes, Banon from Provence, Picodon de Dieulefit washed in white wines are but a few examples.

Wine, the crown jewel of French pride, demands, if not knowledge and experience, then at least a degree of respect. So Balzac was seen to stop a diner who was too quick to down a fine bottle: "This is a wine, my friend, to be caressed with the eyes." "And then?" "Then you breathe it in." "And then?" "You put it back on the table, without touching it, piously." "And then?" "Then you talk about it."

The quality of a wine depends on its *cru* (the vineyard that produced it), its *millésime* (vintage, or year of production) and its *appellation* (AOC: *appellation d'origine contrôlée*, reserved for fine wines from a particular clearly defined area; VDQS, *vin délimité de qualité supérieure*, used for region wines often of excellent quality; and vin de pays, the most modest *appellation*, but which includes many honest products that have been elaborated with care). "Table wines" offer no guarantees whatsoever. They are often haphazard blends of the least appealing products the vines have to offer.

When it comes to tasting a wine, its age is a determining factor. Each wine has its moment of excellence, that must be waited for, but must not be exceeded. Too young, and a wine will not have had the time to develop its qualities. Too old, and these qualities will have disappeared. Other factors include opening the bottle, allowing it to breathe, its serving temperature, and perhaps decanting. If you have any doubt, ask a specialist.

France has six main wine-growing regions. Alsace, Bordeaux, Burgundy, Champagne, Côtes-du-Rhône, and the Loire Valley, to which are added neighboring regions, doubtless less prestigious but often excellent and—thanks to their prices—extremely popular.

Alsace produces mostly spicy white wines, from simple light wines (Sylvaner, Pinot blanc) to fruitier wines (Pinot gris, Gewurztraminer, muscat), by way of the Riesling, a fine grape variety with a well-deserved reputation. The *vendanges tardives* or late harvest wines, made from grapes left on the vine until the first frost, are magnificent, rich in natural sugars and fragrance (not to mention high in price, and rightly so). Let's not forget the Crémant, a sparkling wine made in the same way champagne is, and Pinot Noir, the only red grown in the region.

Bordeaux country, which has exported its wines to northern Europe since the 13th century, benefits from an incomparable reputation. It should be noted that only a handful of the *châteaux* mentioned on the labels actually refer to an aristocratic home, or even a particular vineyard. The word is merely a term used for commercial purposes. Along side the *crus classés* representing some of the most sought after and costliest wines in the world, Bordeaux offers more affordable *crus bourgeois*, and *crus artisans* that are modest but often of fine quality.

The main wines of Bordeaux are the prestigious red médocs (Médoc, Haut-médoc, Moulis, Listrac, Margaux, Saint-Julien, Pauillac, Saint-Estèphe), plus Saint-Émilion, Pomerol and Lalande-de-pomerol, excellent Fronsacs, Graves, and remarkable reds and whites from Pessac-Léognan. Reputed sweet wines include Sauternes and Barsacs, and Loupiacs that are a little gentler on the pocketbook. And then there are the Côtes (de Bordeaux, de Francs, de Castillon, de Blaye, and especially de Bourg) and the plain whites from Entre-DDeux-Mers. Beware of generic appellations like Bordeaux, Bordeaux blanc sec or Bordeaux Supérieur.

We should mention in passing the noteworthy, hearty wines of the neighboring South West region, among which Bergerac, Gaillac (one of the oldest wines in France), Cahors (another wine whose roots go back to antiquity), and the Côtes of the region (de Duras, de Buzet, du Marmandais, and du Frontonnais). Moving further south towards the Pyrénées, there are remarkable red Madirans, white Pacherencs, marvelous white jurançons both dry and sweet, Tursan from the Landes and Irouléguy from Basque Country.

Burgundy, dear to Colette who was an experienced diner and gourmande, is a symbol of elegance. The whites from Chablis, the most copied in the world, are incomparable after years of aging. The legendary wines of the Côtes-de-Nuits, Gevrey-chambertin, Vosne-Romanée, Clos de Vougeot, Chambolle-Musigny, Nuits-Saint Georges do not overshadow those of the Côte de Beaune, the hefty Cortons and Pommards and the tender wines of Savigny, Volnay and Beaune. In the 14th century, the red wines of Beaune were reserved for the aristocracy, the king, and the pope! As for the Tâche, Montrachet and Romané-Conti wines, they have become veritable myths, the symbol of the finest and the most accomplished products that the art of wine making can offer.

Down from the slopes, we continue our tour. Southern Burgundy produces attractive wines, obviously less prestigious but also more affordable. Excellent whites from the Côte Chalonnaise like Rully, Mercurey, Givry, and Montagny, plus those of the Mâconnais: Mâcon, Saint-Véran, the elegant Pouilly-Fuissé, Pouilly-Loché, and Pouilly-Vinzelles.

It would be ungracious to forget, to the east of Burgundy, the wines from the Jura: Arbois, Côtes-du-Jura, and Château-Chalon, king of the *vins jaunes* or heady yellow wines, and the ever surprising *Vin de paille*, a rare sweet wine known as the wine for women who have just given birth.

In all French vineyards, the harvest takes place in the fall. Here, grapes are hand picked in the traditional way.

Further south, the wines from the Savoy and Bugey are not well known, but some, like the seyssel, are nervous and distinctive.

And above all, between Burgundy and Côtes-du-Rhône, the beloved Beaujolais, red or white, and its ten *crus*: Saint-Amour, Juliénas, Moulin-à-vent, Chénas, Fleurie, Chiroubles, Morgon, Régnié, Côte de Brouilly, and Brouilly. The names ring out like a lively dance at a Bastille Day ball.

The wine cellars of many producers are architectural wonders, like the Chartreux cellars in the Jura region, with its medieval vaulted ceilings, pictured here.

Champagne is probably the most famous wine-growing region in the world. Claims that Dom Pérignon, wine keeper at the Hautvilliers Abbey in the 18th century, invented the sparkling wine are not entirely accurate, for it existed empirically (it was talked about as early as Henri IV's time), but he developed the precise techniques that give the wine its unique characteristics. Champagne making is an art of blending and maintaining consistent taste. Only some of the production is vintage, and then only in the best years. The categories of *brut*, *sec* or *demi-sec* (extra dry to semi-sweet) depend on the amount of sugar compound added to ferment the wine and reduce acidity. Rosé Champagne is obtained by adding a few drops of red wine to a white base, or by fermenting still rosé wine. Many prestigious champagne houses have been sold to large industrial conglomerates, but some independent houses, which stake their business on quality, have managed to resist the powerful groups. The best known and most expensive champagnes are not always synonymous with excellence. Trust a specialist, and your own taste buds.

The Côtes-du-Rhône, from Vienne to Avignon, is the second French wine-growing region after Bordeaux. In the vicinity of Vienne excellent wines are produced, including the very old red Côte-Rôtie and the whites Condrieu and Château-Grillet. The region of Valence provides red and white Saint-Joseph and Cornas, which can be of very high quality, the venerable hermitage and Crozes-Hermitage, and white Saint-Péray. Between Montélimar and Avignon, next to the heterogeneous productions from Côtes-du-Rhône, Côtes-du-Rhône-villages, and du-Ventoux, Costières-de-Nîmes or Coteaux-du-Tricastin, are found the justly renowned Châteauneuf-du-Pape, the lovely but less popular Gigondas, and Vacqueyras, delicious lirac in reds, whites, and rosés, and tavel, a charming rosé. This too is where Muscat-de-Beaumes-de-Venise and Rasteau Rancio are produced, two sheer delights.

The vineyards of the Languedoc-Roussillon supply 40 percent of wine drunk in France. Quality, generally mediocre a century ago, has notably improved, especially among the reds.

In the South East, towards the Italian border, Provence offers along with a range of spicy whites and rosés or delicious reds like Bandol, a highly irregular production that encompasses the best and the worst of wines. But with a little patience and curiosity, one can always find a few good bottles wherever one looks.

Finally, Corsica meets expectations with its reds that are high in tannin, its aromatic whites and fruity rosés.

The Loire, from the Massif Central to the Atlantic, is fertile ground for vineyards. Pouilly-sur-Loire, Pouilly-Fumé, Sancerre (that good King Henri IV considered to be the finest wine in the kingdom), Menetou-Salon (enjoyed by Jacques Cœur in the 15th century) Quincy, and Reuilly, available in whites, but also reds and rosés. Along with the three colors of mass-produced Touraine, reds from Chinon, Bourgueil and Saint-Nicolas-de-Bourgueil, whites from Montlouis and Vouvray (the latter had its praises sung by Rabelais and Balzac), still, sparkling or sweet, shine over the Touraine region

with legendary brilliance. The Saumurois and Anjou regions can be proud of the Saumur-Champigny, exquisite whites from Savennières, and the noble *liquoreux*, before making way for the Muscadet from the Pays Nantais of which the more highly prized is the Sèvre-et-Maine.

Wine is not supposed to quench thirst but to exalt a dish, making their marriage an unforgettable experience. Without wine, the best of meals will be lopsided. That is why each recipe here also includes a suggestion of a region or a *cru* that the chefs feel will make the best accompaniment. But there is no such thing as just one perfect match, since taste, however informed and cultivated, is a subjective, personal, intimate experience and for every recommendation, there are countless exceptions. Your own experiments will be your best guide. As a rule of thumb, there is little chance of going wrong by serving a dish and a wine from the same geographic region. An area's cuisine develops around its vineyards, kitchens, and wine cellars and it tries to strike a balance between the subtlety and the heartiness of a dish and the strength of a wine. Of all the virtues of the French, balance is the most desirable and the key to the art of gastronomy.

The owner of this wine shop spends as much energy preserving the traditional appearance of his business as he does defending small, quality wine producers.

Part Two: Cooking in Paris

Between high technology and plain old ingenuity

You probably have a refrigerator at your disposal a stove with four burners, and an oven with a broiler or grill. But even with just a small fridge and a couple of electric rings, you will be able to cook most of the recipes here.

Remember, you can cook well with nothing more than a good paring knife, a couple of spoons or spatulas, a colander, a pot or two and a skillet or frying pan. If we may be allowed to paraphrase, a good workman has good tools, but a good workman also knows how to improvize and adapt to any situation.

French kitchen knives are highly regarded all over the world and can be purchased from specialty stores and online stores. As well as a few small sharp paring knives, you will need one large one for chopping. And don't forget a good knife sharpener and a solid cutting board. Wooden cutting boards tend to absorb fish flavors so either cover with clingfilm or use a plastic cutting board. Kitchen shears, a vegetable peeler, zester, garlic press, and cherry or olive pitter (stoner) are also essential. In terms of high technology equipment, you need loook no further than an electric beater (or whisk), a food mill, and a food processor, blender or liquidizer, an electric grinder, and an electric grater with different blades including a mandolin for slicing (a manual grater is just as good though).

Probably the most famous French kitchen utensils found throughout the world are the cast iron and enamel cooking pots. A good cast iron, ovenproof pot with a lid is essential for preparing many Parisian dishes, as are cast iron (non-stick) skillets. A large, shallow sauteuse is useful but not essential. You will need a variety of baking dishes and ramekins for soufflés and gratins.

For baking desserts, invest in some cake pans, spring form pans, pastry circles, and oven mitts!

Other basic kitchen utensils include a set of measuring cups and weighing scales, a pastry brush, pointed sieve (also called a chinois or china cup), a large strainer or colander, salad spinner, several mixing bowls, baking paper, foil, paper towels (kitchen roll), and a large needle and kitchen twine. Before starting a recipe, check the equipment it requires. And if you do not have everything stated, decide how you are going to improvize before starting!

Opposite:
Some common utensils found in any Parisian kitchen.

This page:
(Clockwise from left): A garlic press, food mill, and cast iron pot.

French Ingredients

*An on-going quest
for freshness and quality*

FRUIT AND VEGETABLES

APPLES: The favorite fruit of the French. Varieties found in France include clochard, Granny Smith, reine de reinettes, Canada, Cox, golden, and elstar. Use them cooked or raw, choosing varieties that keep their shape or cook down, depending on the needs of the recipe.

APRICOTS (summer): Choose them for flavor, not size. Use ripe when the flesh is tender, raw or cooked.

ARTICHOKES (summer, autumn): Use the large *camus de Bretagne* or other green globe varieties for the hearts; use *poivrades* or *violets* from Provence which can practically be eaten whole, raw or cooked.

ASPARAGUS (spring, early summer): wild, green or white, they have very different flavors and are only used cooked.

BELL PEPPERS: Also known as capsicum. At their best in summer, bell peppers come in green, red or yellow. Served raw or cooked.

BERRIES (late spring, summer): Blackberries, blueberries, cherries, currants (red or black), raspberries, and strawberries are marvelous in season, insipid in the winter.

CABBAGE (late spring, summer): Included here are Brussels sprouts (cooked), red, white, and green Savoy cabbages, but also broccoli and cauliflower (used raw or cooked).

CELERY: The stalks should have the fibrous outer leaves removed and can be used raw or cooked.

CELERY ROOT (celeriac): A dense sphere, with ivory colored flesh, it is used cooked.

CITRUS FRUIT: **Lemons** (all seasons) are most commonly used fresh, they are also sold preserved in brine; **limes** (all seasons) are more exotic in origin and very different in taste; the best **oranges** (winter) are Maltese or navel; **grapefruit** may be yellow (all seasons) or pink (winter); **mandarin oranges** and **tangerines** (in France, people prefer those from Corsica) are simple winter desserts. French cuisine makes great use of citrus fruit. Choose untreated ones, especially if you plan to use the zest.

CUCUMBER: Pick ones that are not too big or they will be full of seeds. Ensure that they are firm from end to end. In most varieties, the skin can be eaten but occasionally it is bitter and should be peeled. Used raw and more rarely cooked.

DRIED BEANS or PULSES: **Green lentils** from Le Puy, **white haricot beans** including the ones from Soissons, **split peas** and **garbanzo beans** (chick peas) are all nourishing and

Artichokes

Eggplant

Savoy cabbage

Fennel

Pineapple

Lentils

Pumpkin

filling and are mostly cooked in the winter.

DRIED FRUIT: Apricots and figs from Turkey, dates, sultanas, and dark or golden currants are a veritable bounty in the winter months. The French also consider nuts to be dried fruits and use walnuts, hazelnuts, pine nuts, and pistachios widely.

EGGPLANT (summer): Also known as aubergine. Pick eggplants that are not too large, firm, with smooth, shiny skins and bright green stems. Use cooked.

FAVA BEANS (spring, summer): Also known as broad beans. Removing their thick pods and tough skins requires patience (see page 46). Allow 1 lb (500 g) per person, unshelled. Usually cooked, occasionally eaten raw.

FENNEL (autumn, winter): Select round, dense, white bulbs with bright green stems. Discard the outer layers. Use raw or cooked.

LEEK: choose the thin-stalked variety known as *"baguette."* Usually only the white is eaten; eaten cooked.

LETTUCE AND SALAD GREENS: Included in many a meal. Dandelion, arugula (rocket), mesclun (a mixture of greens), romaine, lolla, nasturtiums, and zucchini (courgette) flowers in summer, curly endive, batavia, escarole, lamb's lettuce, chicory, watercress, Belgian endive ,and raddicchio in the cold season, and *rougette* or *feuille de chêne* all year long. The art of salad making involves balancing its ingredients and its dressing.

MUSHROOMS: They come farmed like white mushrooms (the only ones that can be used raw)

as well as oyster mushrooms, *pieds-de-mouton* (originally from Japan, they can be used as a substitute for *ceps*), or wild and full-flavored like the *trompettes-de-la-mort, ceps, girolles* (summer and autumn), or morels (spring). The *nec plus ultra* is of course the truffle, white or black. Very costly, but incomparable, it can be used raw or cooked.

PEARS: The juiciest, most flavorful varieties are Williams, *beurré*-Hardy or *doyenné-du-comice.* Used raw or cooked.

POTATOES: The most popular vegetable in France. Varieties available include bintje, BF15, ratte, roseval and charlotte. Choose waxy ones that hold their shape or floury ones that mash easily when cooked depending on the requirements of the recipe.

PUMPKIN (spring, summer): One of a number of orange fleshed squash (marrow) with subtly different textures and tastes. Used cooked.

SPINACH: The leaves, often caked with soil, must be carefully washed and trimmed (see page 56). When used cooked, count 1 lb (500 g) per person unprepared spinach. Young leaves are also eaten raw.

SWISS CHARD: Choose ones that are small and tender, with clear white stems and green leaves. Large ones are fibrous and dry. Eat cooked.

TOMATOES (summer): Avoid industrially produced, greenhouse or canned types, and choose them in season and grown on the vine. In winter, you might consider ones imported from warm lands like Tunisia and Morocco. They can be used raw or cooked, generally peeled and seeded. Drop them into boiling water for 10 seconds, then under running cold water. The skin will slip off easily. Remove the stem and the tough core, cut in half horizontally. Use your thumb to scrape out seeds...it's as easy as that!

TROPICAL FRUIT: Bananas, kiwis, mangoes, papayas, pineapple, star fruit...whenever possible, choose fruit that was picked ripe in its country of origin and shipped by air for freshness.

VEGETABLES, EARLY, ALSO NEW OR BABY: Found in the spring, always small in size, often sold in bunches with their leaves or stems still attached, many vegetables are sold "new" including carrots, turnips, onions, peas, green beans, snow peas (mange-tout), and potatoes. In French markets, "*primeur*" vegetables are the very first harvests of the year, whatever the season.

ZUCCHINI (spring, summer): Choose zucchini (courgettes) that are small, dense and firm. Use cooked, or raw, finely sliced in salads.

HERBS, SPICES, AND CONDIMENTS

BOUQUET GARNI: A classic mixture of sprigs of herbs (parsley, thyme, bay leaves), tied into a bundle. Adds taste to boiled and stewed dishes.

GARLIC: At its best when it is young, in the spring and summer. Out of season, remove the sprout in the middle that is hard on the digestion.

HERBS: Avoid at all costs dried or powdered herbs (the rare exceptions to this rule are bay leaves,

thyme, origano, and rosemary). Use them fresh in season, bought in bunches from the market, or grown in a pot or in a corner of the garden. The most common ones are basil, chervil, chives, cilantro (coriander), dill, mint (sweet or pepper), parsley (flat leaf, whenever possible, curly, when not), tarragon. French cookery uses great amounts of herbs.

Tomatoes on the vine

HORSERADISH: A white-fleshed root vegetable, with a very strong flavor. It is sold in jars, ready to use. Mixed with whipped cream, it makes an excellent sauce for smoked fish.

MUSTARD: There are all kinds. The world famous Dijon is refined, pale, and strong. From Meaux, also called "*à l'ancienne*" it contains whole seeds.

OLIVES: Green, black or violet, buy them with the pits (stones) in, for more taste.

Garlic

ONION: They come in yellow (the most common variety), white, and sweet red onion, and *grelot* (or pearl) onions. One of the most widely used flavorings in French cooking. Careful, they can make you cry! Peel them under running water. Scallions (also called spring onions), are used throughout the spring and summer.

SALT: Marsh salt, harvested by hand and packed unprocessed without any chemical additives, is the nec plus ultra. Ground it is called fleur de sel, in larger pieces, it is known as rock salt. Both retain a little moisture. The most famous is from Guérande in Brittany, with a pronounced flavor of iodine and seaweed.

Shallots

SHALLOTS: Long (Jersey) types are best. They also come in yellow and rosy varieties. Widely used is sauces. When spouted, they are called cives in

Esplette chilies

Onions

Olives

Fleur de sel *(sea salt)*

Phyllo pastry

French, and are used like scallions.

SPICES: anise seed, celery salt, chili (tiny, very strong peppers from the West Indies, *espelette* from Basque Country, and Cayenne pepper), cinnamon (in sticks or ground), cloves (the head of which contains all the flavor), coriander seeds, curry powder (the best mixes are Indian brands, available mild, medium or hot, depending on the amount of chili), fennel, ginger (the fresh rhizome is peeled and grated, also available powdered or candied), juniper berries, nutmeg (whole, then grated as needed), paprika (pick the mild variety from Hungary), pepper (mild white, strong black, or mixed, it must be freshly ground as needed, finely or coarsely—the latter is called mignonette; there are also fruity, green peppercorns, best bought vacuum-packed, or fragrant pink peppercorns), quatre-épices (a blend of ginger, clove, pepper and nutmeg), saffron (in threads or powdered form), vanilla beans, powdered or extract (the Bourbon variety from Reunion, or the rarer, most fragrant kind from Tahiti). Avoid artificial flavorings and use powdered spices with caution, which lose their strength quickly and acquire a taste of sawdust or soap.

GROCERIES

BOUILLON CUBES: Dissolved in water, the cubes add flavor to boiled dishes. Homemade stock can be used, but it is time-consuming.

CHOCOLATE AND COCOA: use "couverture" chocolate or dark chocolate, containing between 55% and 70% cocoa. If using powdered cocoa, pick an unsweetened variety.

COURT-BOUILLON, CUBES OR POWDER: Dissolved in water, it is used for poaching fish. It would take a little too long to make it from scratch.

FLOUR: wheat flour is the most common. For pastries and cakes, sift it before use.

FOND: made from veal, poultry etc. Concentrated stock used as the basis of many sauces and gravies. It is fastidious to make from scratch, but is available ready-to-use forms, including concentrate, liquid and dry (use 1 tablespoon concentrate for 10 cl boiling water).

FOND: made from veal, poultry etc. Concentrated stock used as the basis of many sauces and gravies. It is fastidious to make from scratch, but is available ready-to-use forms, including concentrate, liquid and dry (use 1 tablespoon concentrate to 100 ml boiling water).

GOOSE OR DUCK FAT: excellent cooking fat, especially for sautéing potatoes. Reserved fat from a confit will keep several months, but it can also be bought in jars and cans.

HONEY: The best liquid honey for cooking is acacia honey from Hungary.

OIL: Have at least three types on hand: peanut (neutral, for cooking); olive (tasty, for cooking and salads); and walnut (for salads only). There are also oils of corn, sunflower, hazelnut, and sesame. Be careful, their flavors vary greatly, few can be cooked at high temperatures and many go rancid quite quickly. Peanut or olive oil forms the basis of mayonnaise, one of the most famous sauces in the world, and a classically French recipe. In a mixing bowl, stir together an egg yolk with 1 teaspoon of strong mustard (if liked) or the same amount of oil (if not). Add oil very gradually, stirring constantly with a wooden spoon until a smooth emulsion is reached. The sauce is ready when it is thick and stiff. Add salt to taste, and lighten it with lemon juice. This marvelous sauce is fail-proof, if all the ingredients are at room temperature. If for some reason the sauce separates or curdles, take another egg yolk, and very slowly whisk in the first mixture.

PASTA: Pick Italian pasta, from a reputable brand, and made of durum wheat. Cook in large quantities of water at a rolling boil, and follow the instructions to cook them al dente.

PHYLLO PASTRY OR BRIK: Arab, Turkish or Greek in origin, it makes airy, flaky pastry that cooks quickly and can be used in sweet or savory dishes

RICE: There are 8000 varieties! You can content yourself with three types: superfino arborio from the Po Valley for risotto and desserts (this is the only rice that does not require washing); Basmati or Surinam for plain boiled rice; and a Camargue or Madagascar rice, for recipes *au gras* (cooked in rich broth) or pilafs. Avoid parboiled or converted rice that is totally lacking in taste.

SEMOLINA: Made of wheat for couscous and desserts, of corn for polenta. Follow the instructions on the package.

SUGAR: Refined white sugar is the most common, made from either cane or beets. Confectioners' (icing) sugar (a powder); superfine (caster) sugar; or granulated sugar. Brown or demerara sugars contain varying amounts of molasses. Raw sugar is unrefined.

VINEGAR: There are all kinds. Regard fanciful product with extreme caution. The most dependable are aged red wine vinegar, sherry (xeres) vinegar, balsamic, cider, white (or crystal) vinegar (used only in cooking). Vinegar is the soul of vinaigrette, one of the most famous sauces in the world, invented in France in the 14th century. Dissolve a pinch of salt in one part vinegar, add a few grinds of pepper, then three parts oil and whisk together until emulsified. The secret of success is in the ingredients. Olive oil with balsamic vinegar (or lemon juice) or walnut oil and sherry vinegar, are classics. You can also add a little mustard. With seeds, it picks up wine vinegar and peanut oil. Try it. Also don't neglect cornichons (small pickles or gherkins) or onions pickled in vinegar, that add life to cold cuts and hams.

SEAFOOD AND SHELLFISH

Parisians love seafood, and thanks to quick transport and refrigeration techniques, they can enjoy them year round. Before, eating shellfish was reserved for months with Rs, from September to April, when much seafood is still at its best.
Shellfish available in Paris include: **sea urchins** (eaten raw), **periwinkles** and **whelks** (cooked), **scallops** (cooked, though very rarely also served

Sea urchins

Whelks

Scallops

Oysters

Araignée or rock crab

Lobster

Langoustine

Octopus

raw), flat belon, deep-shelled creuse or fines de claire **oysters** (usually raw, very occasionally cooked), small bouchot **mussels** (cooked) or larger plumper varieties that are served raw or stuffed and cooked on the half shell, palourde, praire or clovisse **clams** (again raw or cooked) and tiny pétoncles or bay **scallops**.

Petit-gris or Burgundy escargots (snails) are land-bound shelled creatures.

The main crustaceans, best when during the warm season, are all eaten cooked: araignées, étrilles (spider or rock) **crabs**, the latter being used for bisques and fish soups, or the more familiar, large tourteau crabs (preferably female), bay or soft-shelled shrimp and jumbo **prawns**, blue-shelled Brittany **lobster**, *langoustine* or Dublin Bay prawns (again preferably from Brittany).

The best freshwater *écrevisse* or crayfish are the red-clawed variety. And finally, in the cephalopoda family, there are exquisite molluscs better known as **octopus**, **cuttlefish**, and **squid**. Prefer smaller ones, and always serve them cooked.

FISH

There are over 20,000 species of fish. We will simply mention a handful that are used in our recipes because they are the most popular in French cooking. Pick fish that is firm-fleshed, shiny without any trace of blood, with bright red gills, shiny, round eyes, and a fresh smell. Avoid pre-cut fillets, and have them cut for you when you order. Exercise great care when cooking fish, for failure to do so can result in ruining a fine product.

BAR: similar to sea bass, it is one of the finest fish, with lean flesh. It is called loup or wolf in the Mediterranean because of its voracious appetite.

BRILL: a flat fish with dense, slightly fatty flesh, related to the turbot.

COD: the most popular fish, with lean, flaky flesh. Cod is sold fresh, but salt cod or morue is also widely used, the best being bacalhão, or "green" cod from Portugal.

DORADE: similar to porgy. Lean and tender, the gray variety of this ocean fish is considered to be better than the pink.

RED MULLET: A small, semi-fatty fish, with distinctive tasting iodized flesh. If it is not available, use the bonier, less valued grondin or gurnard.

SALMON: Look for a wild salmon fished in Scotland or in the Pacific northwest. Failing that, pick a young, farmed fish.

SARDINE: A small fatty fish, equally delicious raw, marinated or cooked.

SOLE: This famous and particularly tasty flat fish belonging to the Pleuronectiforme order has, through the long process of evolution, developed the particularity of having both eyes on the same side of its head.

TUNA: The flesh of this fatty fish resembles veal. Albacore tuna is the finest. If it is no available, use red tuna.

TURBOT: Large Pleuronectiforme with very white flesh. Its excellent reputation is well deserved.

DAIRY PRODUCTS

BUTTER: Sweet (unsalted) or salted (also available semi-salted or *demi-sel* in France). The best sweet butter in France comes from Échiré, Sainte-Mère or Isigny, and the best salted butter from Guérande or Noirmoutier. Be careful! Butter burns easily and should be cooked over low heat. Mixing it with an equal amount of oil allows it to be cooked at slightly higher temperatures. It goes without saying that margarine can in no way replace butter, which French cuisine uses extensively.

CREME FRAICHE: The best is unpasteurized, but pasteurized, more readily available, can also be used. The exquisite nature of this thick cream makes it ideal served with berries or fruit tarts, and it is recommended in cooking, especially in preparing sauces. Heavy (whipping or double) cream is called *fleurette* in French, and is ideal for making whipped cream, which is called chantilly cream when it is sweetened. The secret to making it is putting the cream, the mixing bowl and the whisk or (electric) beaters in the refrigerator an hour before whipping. When ready, whip without stopping until the beaters leave an impression in the cream. Beat it any longer and it will turn into butter, any less and it will be runny. If making chantilly, sprinkle in sugar when the cream has begun to form peaks but is still soft. If only thick *crème fraîche* is available, dilute with a little iced water for the right consistency.

EGGS: Eggs in France are sold at the *cremerie*, along with dairy products (which is as strange as finding rabbit at poultry butchers, as tradition still dictates). Chicken eggs are the most common. Pick them as fresh as possible, ideally laid by grain-fed, free-range chickens. In these and most French recipes, use eggs that are medium in size (about 55–60 g) and bring them to room temperature about 30 minutes before using. Quail eggs are also found, and are often used in appetizers.

MILK: Choose fresh milk—UHT and other extended shelf life products taste of chalk. Use whole milk for desserts. It is tastier and more unctuous.

Crème fraîche

POULTRY

Whether small birds (quail, pigeons) or large farmyard animals (ducks, capons, roosters, turkeys, geese, guinea or game hens, chickens), choose the best available. In France, find ducks from Challans, chickens from the Bourdonnais, Bresse or Sarthe regions, geese from the Touraine. Pick them free-range, grain-fed and at the right age. Avoid at all costs industrially produced animals, even if the price is attractive. It is better to eat a fine product occasionally rather than eating poor quality foods often. Farmed rabbits are also sold by the poultry butcher, an oddity that dates back to the Middle Ages. Under poultry, we also include fresh duck, chicken and rabbit livers, which are wonderful pan-fried with a few salad greens, and *foie gras*, fattened livers of geese (the best of which come from Alsace) or of ducks (from the southwest), as well as magrets (fattened duck breasts), rillettes (seasoned duck or goose meat cooked in its fat, then cooled until spreadable) and confit (whole pieces of meat preserved in

Whipped cream

Quail's eggs

fat), also specialties of the southwest that illustrate masterful skill and patience.

MEAT AND CHARCUTERIE

Nothing can replace the knowledge of a specialist, especially when it comes to something as crucial as meat, the cornerstone of French culinary tradition. All slaughterhouse animals are divided into the noble, expensive cuts that require short cooking times (grilling or roasting), and the cheaper, "lower" cuts, that are slow cooked (boiled, braised or simmered). If an animal has been raised and slaughtered correctly, every cut willbe full of flavor, so long as it is cooked well. We will not discuss game animals here, or horsemeat, simply because one cannot hope to do it all!

LAMB: These days, mutton, thought to be too strong in taste, has been replaced by milk-fed lamb, the flesh of which is pale and tender, unweaned from its mother's milk, or "white" lamb, with dark red meat and very white fat, fed on milk and grass in the open air. The best meat is from Sologne, Sisteron and the Normandy coast (where feeding on the greens salted by the rising tides flavors the meat). The "noble" cuts are the leg of lamb, the saddle, and chops that should be eaten medium rare. Other prized milk-fed animals are piglets (less than two months old) and young male goats, from the Poitou or from Corsica.

VEAL: Its pale pink flesh, with very white fat, is tender and moist. It is served medium. 100% milk-fed veal (said to be "from under the mother" in French) from the Limousin or the Touraine regions is the nec plus ultra. The best cuts are the fillets, the chops and the eye round that the butcher cuts into scallops. Veal offal (liver, sweet-

Lamb
1 Neck
2 Rib and loin
(chops and roast)
3 Shoulder
4 Spareribs
5 Flank
6 Saddle
7 Leg of lamb

Veal
1 Head
2 Neck
3 Chops
4 Shoulder
5 Shank
6 Breast
7 Loin
8 Flank
9 Rump
10 Sirloin
11 Sirloin tip
12 Round

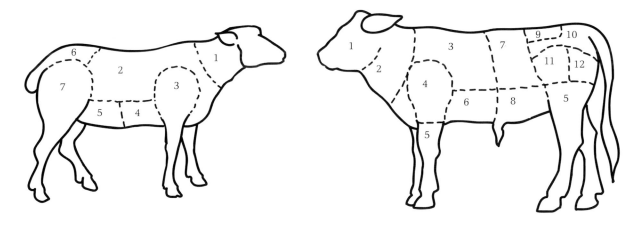

breads, kidneys, tripe, feet and head) are enjoyed by connoisseurs.

BEEF: The meat should be deep red in color, with yellowing fat, and should be well aged, served only two to three weeks after slaughter. Used any earlier and it will render water. If you have bought meat that has not had time to age (light red in color and bloody), you can age it at home. Remove it from its wrapping, place it on a plate, brush with a little oil and leave in the refrigerator for a few days, turning from time to time, so that it will release its water. The quality cuts (tenderloin, rib eye, rib and rump steaks) are eaten rare, or even raw as is the case with steak tartare. The best races for beef in France are the Limousine, Salers, Charolaise and Blonde d'Aquitaine.

PORK: The most affordable of what is erroneously referred to as white meat. The best cuts of fresh pork are the loin, tenderloin and chops. In Alsace, the blade and shoulder are enjoyed salt cured or smoked. Pork is the most valued commodity in producing charcuterie or various forms of dried, cured or preserved meats: cured hams like those from Bayonne (substitute Spanish serrano ham), smoked hams like those from Alsace, or boiled *au torchon* which is the favorite in Paris; fresh sausages like garlic sausages, or dried ones like jésus, rosette de Lyon or dried sausages from Auvergne, cooking sausages like pistachio sausages from Lyon or Morteaux sausages; blood (also called black) pudding or sausage, made with pork fat and onions, *andouilles* from Vire or Guémené, hand-tied *andouillettes* (chitterling sausage), the best being certified by the AAAAA (Amicable Association of Authentic Andouillette Appreciators), rillettes, slated and smoked bacon, trotters, stuffed or plain. The French say that the whole of the pig makes for good eating?

Beef
1 Jowl
2 Neck
3 Blade or chuck roast
4 Ribs
5 Brisket
6 Shank
7 Short ribs
8 Stewing or ground beef (mince)
9 Rib eye
10 Top loin
11 Tenderloin
12 Tip steak or roast
13 Flank steak
14 Sirloin
15 Rolled rump
16 Round steak or roast

Pork
1 Jowl
2 Neck
3 Back fat
4 Blade chops
5 Loin roast
6 Picnic roast
7 (Ham) hock
8 Rib chops and tenderloin
9 Ham
10 Belly and bacon

Part Three: The Recipes

Basic recipes for sauces and dressing
precede those for main dishes, which begin on page 44

Basil Dressing

1 shallot, peeled and finely chopped
2 large white mushrooms, cleaned and
  finely chopped
2 ripe, firm tomatoes, peeled and seeded
  (see page 32), finely chopped
1 handful basil leaves, finely chopped
  (reserve a few whole leaves to garnish)
Juice of 3 lemons
Salt and pepper to taste
1 cup (250 ml) olive oil

Place the shallots, mushrooms, and tomatoes in a mixing bowl, add the finely chopped basil leaves, setting aside a few for decoration. With a fork, whisk the lemon juice, salt, pepper, and oil, and stir into vegetables.

Tomato Sauce

2 tablespoons olive oil
1 clove garlic, peeled and sliced
2 onions, peeled and sliced
1 bouquet garni comprising 3 stalks of parsley,
  1 sprig thyme, and 1 bay leaf
2 lb (1 kg) flavorful tomatoes, peeled, seeded,
  and roughly chopped (see page 32)

Heat the oil in a pan over medium heat, sauté the onion and garlic, stirring often so they do not brown. Add the bouquet garni, tomatoes, salt, and pepper,

Measurements

Measurements in this book are given in volume as far as possible: 1 measuring **cup** contains 250 ml (roughly 8 oz); 1 **teaspoon** contains 5 ml, while 1 **tablespoon** contains 15 ml or the equivalent of 3 teaspoons.

Servings

Unless otherwise stated, all recipes are for 4 people.

Ingredients

When a recipe lists a hard-to-find or an unusual ingredient, see pages 31 and 39 for possible substitutes.

and cook, stirring from time to time, until the mixture thickens, about 30 minutes.

Orange Buerre Blanc Sauce

3 oranges, reserve zest of one orange and juice
  all three
1 glass dry white wine
2 shallots, peeled and finely chopped
1¼ cups (250 g) chilled butter, cubed small

Opposite:
*Wild Asparagus
and Snow Peas
with Poached
Eggs (see recipe,
page 43).*

To make the sauce, combine orange juice, wine, and shallots in a small saucepan. Bring to a boil, reduce heat and reduce until only 1 tablespoon of liquid remains. Over very low heat, gradually whisk butter cubes into the reduced liquid, then finish by adding the zest. This orange beurre blanc sauce—which as you can see takes no effort whatsoever—should be kept warm until you are ready to serve.

Buerre Blanc

$^3/_4$ cup (200 ml) white wine
1 tablespoon white vinegar
1 sprig thyme
1 bay leaf
3 shallots, peeled and finely chopped
Salt
Freshly ground pepper
1 tablespoon heavy (double) cream
$^3/_4$ cup (150 g) butter, at room temperature
Juice of $^1/_2$ lemon

Put the wine and vinegar, the thyme and bay leaf, the shallots, salt, and pepper in a small, non-reactive saucepan. Bring to a boil and, very gently, reduce to 1 tablespoon. Discard the thyme and bay leaf. Switch off the heat and add the cream, then the butter, bit by bit, whisking by hand, and, finally, add the juice of half a lemon. Strain through a chinois or sieve and hold over a simmering double boiler.

Sauce Vierge

Generous pinch of salt
Juice of 2 lemons
Freshly ground pepper
8 tablespoons olive oil
2 tomatoes, peeled, seeded and cut in very
  small dice
1 red onion, peeled and finely chopped
1 shallot, peeled and finely chopped
1 tablespoon black olives, from Nice if possible,
  pitted and sliced into rings

In a non-reactive saucepan, dissolve the salt in the lemon juice, then add pepper and olive oil and whisk together with a fork. Add the remaining ingredients and set aside at room temperature.

Champagne Sauce

4 tablespoons olive oil
5 green asparagus, washed and cut into pieces
2 shallots, peeled and finely chopped
$1^1/_4$ cups (300 ml) Champagne (substitute with
  dry sparkling wine)
2 cups (500 ml) heavy (double) cream
Pinch saffron
$^1/_2$ cup (100 g) unsalted butter, cubed, at room
  temperature

Heat oil in a pan and gently cook asparagus and shallots. Add the champagne then reduce until almost dry. Add the cream, saffron, salt, and pepper and cook very gently for a few more minutes, stirring. Process or blend the sauce, then strain through a chinois or sieve. Return to low heat, whisk in butter cubes, remove from direct heat and reserve in a double boiler.

Red Wine Sauce

3 cups (750 ml) Juliénas, or other red
  Beaujolais, wine
1 shallot, peeled and finely chopped
1 bouquet garni of 1 stalk parsley, 1 sprig
  thyme, and 1 bay leaf
1 tablespoon sugar
Coarsely ground mignonette peppercorns
$1^1/_4$ cups (300 ml) veal fond
$3/_4$ cup (200 ml) carrot juice (fresh is possible)
$2/_3$ cup (125 g) butter

In a saucepan, very gently reduce the wine at a
simmer with the shallots, bouquet garni, sugar,
and a good pinch of mignonette, until about 1 cup
(250 ml) liquid is left. Add the fond, and reduce by
half again. Add the carrot juice and correct the
seasoning. Whisk in the butter, a little at a time.
Strain through a chinois or sieve and keep warm
in the top of a simmering double boiler.

Aspergues Sauvaes et Pois Gourmands
aux Oeufs Mollets
Wild Asparagus and Snow Peas with Poached
Eggs (Catherine Guerraz, Chez Catherine)

1 bunch wild asparagus (or baby green
  asparagus), tough stems discarded, tied
  in a bundle
13 oz (400 g) snow peas (*mange-tout*),
  threads removed
4 cups (1 liter) water
2 tablespoons white vinegar
4 eggs
1 tomato, peeled (see page 32), dipped in
  iced water, deseeded and diced
Zest of 1 lemon (removed with a peeler and
cut into thin strips), blanced and refreshed
  in iced water
$1/_3$ cup (30 g) parmesan, shaved
A little chervil and some chives

Vinaigrette

2 tablespoons balsamic vinegar
Salt and freshly ground black pepper to taste
4 tablespoons peanut (groundnut) oil

Cook asparagus and snow peas in salted, boiling
water for 5 minutes. Taste the vegetables, they
should still be firm. Drain and plunge into a bowl
of iced water so that they will stay green until you
are ready to serve. Drain again. Set aside.

To make a vinaigrette, whisk together with a fork
the balsamic vinegar, salt, pepper, and oil in a bowl.
Set this aside, too.

Just before serving, bring the water to a simmer
in a shallow pan, and add the white vinegar. Break
an egg into a bowl, then carefully slip it into
the water. The water should simmer, not boil!
Cook for 4 minutes, remove with a slotted spoon
and drain on paper towel (kitchen roll). Do the same
for the three remaining eggs.

On pretty plates, arrange the asparagus in a circle
around the edges, place the peas in the center and an
egg on top. Sprinkle with chopped tomato, lemon zest,
shaved parmesan, and finish with the vinaigrette.

Garnish this coolly stunning dish with sprigs of
chervil and chives, and accompany with a white
Mâcron or a Savennières (photograph on page 40).

LÉGUMES PRINTANIERS MARINÉS À LA CORIANDRE

Spring Vegetables Marinated in Coriander (Flora Mikula, Les Olivades)

Set aside an hour the night before serving, or in the morning if you are serving this dish in the evening, to give the vegetables enough time to marinate.

 2 cups (500 ml) dry white wine
 2 cups (500 ml) freshly squeezed lemon juice
  (5 to 10 lemons, depending on size)
 1 cup (250 ml) olive oil
 1 tablespoon coriander seeds
 1 sprig thyme
 1 teaspoon salt
 1 bunch green asparagus, washed stems
  removed
 1 bunch baby (new) carrots, peeled and
  washed, retain a little of the green stem
 $6\frac{1}{2}$ oz (200 g) fresh button mushrooms, base
  of stems trimmed, brushed clean
 $6\frac{1}{2}$ oz (200 g) scallion (spring onion)
  bulbs, peeled
 1 bunch fresh cilantro (coriander) leaves
  and stems

Bring the wine and lemon juice to a boil in a saucepan, then add the oil, coriander seeds, thyme, and salt.

Cook each vegetable separately in this mixture, making sure they remain firm. Cook the asparagus and the mushrooms for 5 minutes; the carrots and onions for 10 minutes. Remove them with a slotted spoon and set aside in a serving bowl.

When the vegetables are done, boil the liquid until reduced by half, then pour onto the vegetables and leave to marinate at room temperature.

When you are ready to serve, decorate with fresh cilantro leaves. This refreshing appetizer is an adaptation of the classic vegetables *à la grecque*. Accompany with a white Cassis.

BAVAROISES DE TOMATES, SAUCE BASILIC

Tomato Bavarois with Basil Dressing (Catherine Guerraz, Chez Catherine)

Remember that the bavaroises need a few hours to chill and set. Prepare them in the morning if serving in the evening, or the night before. Finish them just before serving. This recipe serves 8 (it's not worth the trouble to make less).

> 1 teaspoon olive oil
> 1 medium onion, peeled and minced
> 5 ripe, firm tomatoes, peeled (see page 32) and chopped
> 3 cloves garlic, peeled and sliced
> 1 tablespoon tomato paste (concentrate)
> 1 sprig thyme
> 1 bay leaf
> Pinch salt
> 1 tablespoon balsamic vinegar
> 3 sheets gelatin softened with a little cold water, or 1 tablespoon powdered gelatin
> 1 cup (250 ml) heavy (double) cream
> Basil Dressing (see page 41)

Heat 1 tablespoon oil over low heat and sauté the onion. Add the chopped tomato, garlic, tomato paste, thyme, bay leaf, and a generous pinch of salt. Let the mixture reduce gently for 20 minutes. Stir occasionally with a wooden spoon. Once the vegetables have cooked, remove the thyme and bay leaf, force the tomato mixture through a sieve. Add the vinegar and the gelatin (squeeze the sheets dry if used), mix very thoroughly and cool to room temperature. While it is cooling, place the bowl, whisk, and cream in the refrigerator.

When the tomato mixture is cool but not set, beat the cream until firm (see page 37) and fold it in carefully. Fill 8 ramekins and chill until set.

Before serving, prepare the Basil Dressing (see page 41) and stir it into the vegetables. To serve, unmold the baravoises onto individual plates, surround with sauce and garnish with a basil leaf. It would be hard to make it any prettier. Accompany with a white or rosé Cassis.

RAGOUT DE FEVES A LA CORIANDRE, OEUF CASSE

Coriander Fava Bean Ragout with a "Broken" Egg (Christian Etchebest, Le Troquet)

4 lb (2 kg) fava (broad) beans
2 tablespoons olive oil
1 onion, peeled and thinly sliced
1 carrot, peeled and thinly sliced
3½ oz (100 g) smoked bacon, skinned
   and cubed
4 eggs
2 tablespoons white vinegar (for poaching
   the eggs)
1 bunch fresh cilantro (coriander)

Sauce

2 tablespoons balsamic vinegar
6 tablespoons olive oil
1 tablespoon coriander seeds, slightly crushed
Salt
Freshly ground pepper

Shell the fava beans, blanch for 3 minutes in salted boiling water, drain, and rinse in cold water. Cut the skin of each bean and pop the bean out. The process is a little fussy, but worth the trouble. Set beans aside in a cool place.

To make the sauce, combine all the ingredients in a bowl and mix well. Set aside.

Heat the oil in a skillet, sauté the onion for 2 minutes, then add the carrots and bacon and cook for further 5 minutes, stirring often with a wooden spoon. All of this can be done in advance.

Just before serving, poach the eggs (see page 43). Reheat the onion, carrot, and bacon gently, add the beans to warm them slightly, remove from heat and add 4 tablespoons of the vinaigrette. Mix, taste and correct seasoning with salt and pepper, if needed.

Arrange the bean ragoût in four soup plates, place a poached egg atop each plate, pour over the remaining vinaigrette, and sprinkle with fresh cilantro leaves.

At the very last moment, pierce each egg with the tip of a knife so that the yolk seeps out. Accompany with a white Irouléguy.

SOUPE DE POISSON

Fish Soup (Philippe Tredgeu, Chez Casimir)

There is a choice of two garnishes for this soup: croutous or cream—both are equally delicious.

> **Trimmings from 4 dorades (porgies),**
> **i.e. the heads, bones and tails normally**
> **discarded once the fish have been cleaned,**
> **scaled, and filleted; ask your fishmonger**
> **for the same amount of trimmings from**
> **other fish like sole and dab (lemon sole)**
> **or whatever he has readily available.**
> **1 small can tomato paste (concentrate)**
> **4 large cloves garlic**
> **1 bouquet garni comprising 4 stems of flat-leaf**
> **parsley, 1 sprig thyme, and 1 bay leaf**
> **2 small chilies**
> **1 handful sea salt crystals**
> **12 black and white peppercorns**
> **4 cups (1 liter) cold water**

Crouton Garnish

> **2 slices stale bread, cubed**
> **2 tablespoons olive oil**
> **$^{1}/_{3}$ cup (25 g) parmesan, shaved**
> ***Fleur de sel* (salt crystals)**

Cream Garnish

> **Pinch saffron**
> **1 clove garlic**
> **$^{1}/_{2}$ cup (125 ml) heavy (double) cream**
> **Pinch salt**

Put all the soup ingredients in a large pot, bring to a boil and leave to simmer, covered, for 1 hour. When it has cooked, blend the soup in a food processor on its finest setting.

While the soup is cooking, prepare either garnish, as you prefer. If you have settled on croutons, fry the bread in a little olive oil over low heat until golden, them place directly in the soup plates, sprinkle with *fleur de sel* and add a few shavings of parmesan. If you choose the cream, beat until firm (see page 37) with saffron (for color and flavor), garlic, and salt. At the last minute, using a spoon dipped in hot water, float a dollop of cream on each serving of steaming hot soup.

Even when served with such refinement, this sublime dish costs next to nothing. Money does not make for good cooking, only skill and a little creativity do. Accompany with a white Cassis.

Helpful hint: If you have made a tomato *bavaroise* or *tartare* (pages 46 and 62) the day before, add the unused skins and seeds to the tomato paste.

SOUPE GLACEE DE CONCOMBRES, MENTHE ET PAPRIKA

Cold Cucumber, Mint, and Paprika Soup
(Stéphane Baron, Le Zéphyr)

3 slender, firm cucumbers, with shiny skins
1 bunch of mint, green or peppermint, depending on your taste, washed and patted dry
2 large shallots, peeled and chopped
$^1/_2$ cup (125 ml) fresh whole milk
$^1/_2$ cup (125 ml) heavy (double) cream
1 level tablespoon strong Dijon mustard
Drizzle of sherry vinegar
Pinch salt
Pinch freshly ground pepper
Pinch paprika

At least 1 hour before mealtime, wash the cucumbers, cut them in half lengthwise without peeling them, remove the seeds by scraping the center with a little spoon, chop the cucumber and place in a food processor. Wash, pat dry the mint, and add $^3/_4$ of the leaves to the cucumber, together with the shallots, milk, cream, mustard, vinegar, salt, and pepper. Process until smooth, correct seasoning if necessary, and chill until serving.

When ready, whisk the soup lightly, pour four equal servings into soup bowls, and garnish with the remaining chopped reserved mint leaves and a sprinkling of paprika for color and taste.

SOUPE CREMEUSE D'ASPERGES VERTES, OEUF DE CAILLE, PANCETTA

Green Asparagus, Quail Egg, and Pancetta Cream Soup
(Christian Etchebest, Le Troquet)

You can make this soup in advance, reheat it or serve it cold, as you like. Another convenient thing about this recipe is that the asparagus does not have to be peeled. Just rinse and cut off a little of the tough stem.

3 tablespoons olive oil
1 medium onion, peeled and finely chopped
3 bunches green asparagus, tough stems discarded, tips removed, stalks sliced
1 Bayonne ham end (substitute with any other dry cured ham)
1 sprig thyme
1 bay leaf
2 chicken bouillon cubes
4 cups (1 liter) water
Pinch salt
Pinch freshly gound pepper
Scant $^1/_2$ cup (100 ml) heavy (double) cream
1 slice of country bread sliced into small croutons
4 slices pancetta (substitute with smoked bacon)
4 quail eggs
1 bunch chives, chopped

Heat 1 tablespoon of the olive oil over low heat and sauté the onion. Add the sliced asparagus stalks and cook for five minutes, stirring with a wooden spoon. Add the ham, thyme, bay leaf, bouillon cubes, and water, bring to a boil, then reduce to a simmer, 45 minutes. Discard the thyme, bay leaf, and ham, then put the rest through the food processor and sieve. Season with salt

SOUPE GLACÉE DE TOMATES AU BASILIC

Cold Tomato and Basil Soup

(Flora Mikula, Le Olivades)

6 lb (3 kg) tomatoes on the vine,
  very ripe
1 red bell pepper (capsicum), washed,
  seeded, and roughly chopped
$^1/_2$ onion, peeled and cut in half
1 stalk celery, washed and chopped
7 cloves garlic, peeled
$^1/_2$ bunch of basil
1 sprig thyme
1 bay leaf
2 tablespoons superfine (caster)
  sugar
Pinch salt
Pinch freshly ground pepper
A few drops Tabasco, optional
4 tablespoons olive oil

Tapenade

4 slices bread
5 oz (150 g) black
  olives, pitted
1 oz (30 g) salted
  anchovies
1 clove
  garlic,
  peeled
3 table-
  spoons
  olive oil

and pepper, add cream, and mix again. If you opt for hot soup, reheat just before serving.

However you choose to serve it, just before sitting down, pan-fry the croutons in 1 tablespoon of the oil until golden; broil (grill) the pancetta in the oven until crisp (about 3 to 5 mintues); and fry the eggs in the reamining oil in a pan until the white is set. Garnish each soup bowl with an egg, a slice of pancetta, a few asparagus tips, and a scattering of croutons. In a soup tureen, serve the soup topped with chopped chives. This soup is deceptively suave.

To prepare this soup, first preheat the oven to 300°F (150°C, gas 2) on the night before, or on the morning of the evening meal. In a baking dish, place the tomatoes, bell pepper, onion, and celery. Wash and pat dry the basil, remove the leaves and set aside in a dish towel, add a few of the stems to the vegetables in the baking dish, along with 5 of the garlic cloves, the thyme, and the bay leaf. Sprinkle with sugar and salt, then cover with aluminum foil. Bake for $2\frac{1}{2}$ hours. Cool.

When the vegetable compote is ready, put it through a food processor, then force through a sieve, pressing and stirring until all that is left in the sieve is a fibrous, nearly dry residue that you can discard. Taste the soup, correct the salt if needed, add the pepper and Tabasco, if used. Cool to room temperature, then leave in refrigerator until serving. In the meantime, make some basil oil by blending the remaining 2 cloves of garlic, the reserved basil leaves and the oil in the food processor. When everyone has been seated around the table, you can drizzle this fragrant oil directly on the soup in an attractive pattern.

Also, serve a *tapenade*, or olive paste, on the side. Mix all the ingredients (except for bread) until smooth in food processor. Just before serving, spread this delicious condiment on the toasted bread, cut into quarters and serve with the soup.

CREME DE LENTILLES

Cream of Lentil Soup

$6\frac{1}{2}$ (200 g) lentils, preferably from Le Puy, soaked in cold water for 2 hours, drained
1 carrot, peeled and chopped
1 onion, peeled and chopped
1 bouquet garni comprising 4 stalks parsley, 1 sprig thyme, and 1 bay leaf
2 chicken bouillon cubes, mixed in 4 cups (1 liter) boiling water to make a stock, cooled
Pinch salt
Pinch freshly ground pepper
1 knob butter, cut into small pieces

Cream Garnish

$\frac{1}{2}$ cup (125 ml) heavy (double) cream
$\frac{1}{3}$ cup (40 g) chopped hazelnuts

Crouton Garnish

2 slices of stale bread, cubed
2 tablespoons butter
Pinch salt

Place the drained lentils in a pot. Add the carrot and onion, the *bouquet garni*, and the cold bouill on. Skim when it reaches a boil, then cover and simmer for 1 hour. Add salt halfway through (but not much, the bouillon already contains salt). When the lentils are done, put through a food processor and then sieve the soup. Add a hint of pepper and the butter pieces, mix and serve with the garnish of your choice.

Prepare the garnish when the soup is almost ready. If you have chosen the cream, beat it until stiff (see page 37), then add the nuts and, at the last minute, gently place a dollop of cream on the surface of each soup bowl using a spoon dipped in hot water. If you prefer croutons, fry the bread in butter over low heat until golden, sprinkle with salt, then add to the cream of lentils.

SOUPE A L'OIGNON GRATINEE

French Onion Soup

$^1\!/_4$ **cup (50 g) butter**
8 oz (250 g) yellow onions
$2^1\!/_2$ **tablespoons (25 g) flour**
3 chicken bouillon cubes, mixed in
    6 cups ($1^1\!/_2$ liters) boiling water
    to make a stock
Stale bread, preferably *baguette*
$^3\!/_4$ **cup (100 g) freshly grated**
    emmenthal cheese

Over medium heat, melt the butter, and, when it starts to foam, add the onions, then cook, stirring with a wooden spoon, until they begin to color. Sprinkle with flour and stir—it should be a rich golden color. Pour in the boiling stock, stir and leave to simmer 10 minutes, stirring from time to time.

Pour the soup into an ovenproof tureen (better still, into 4 individual soup bowls). Cover the surface with slices of baguette or other bread, cover with the cheese and broil (grill) in the oven until golden.

Traditionally, this legendary soup is designed to comfort night owls and those who work at night.

FLANS DE POTIRON AUX POMMES ET AUX NOISETTES

Pumpkin Flans with Apples and Hazelnuts (Stéphane Baron, Le Zéphyr)

2 lb (1 kg) pumpkin (or butternut squash)
1 chicken bouillon cube
³/₄ cup (200 ml) boiling water
³/₄ cup (200 ml) heavy (double) cream
Pinch salt
Pinch freshly ground pepper
Pinch cayenne pepper
6 eggs
1 large Granny Smith apple (or any other tart,
    cooking apple), washed, quartered, cored,
    and finely diced

Vinaigrette
¹/₃ cup (50 g) chopped hazelnuts
1 ¹/₄ tablespoons butter
Juice of half a lemon
2 tablespoons aged sherry vinegar
4 tablespoons corn, sesame, or sunflower oil
4 tablespoons hazelnut (or walnut) oil

Peel and seed the pumpkin, cut the flesh into chunks, place in a pot, just cover with cold water, bring to a boil, then immediately drain the vegetables you have just blanched.

You can use the same pot to prepare the bouillon with the boiling water. Add the cream, drained pumpkin, salt, pepper, and cayenne pepper. Cook over medium heat for 20 minutes, stirring constantly, until the pumpkin becomes a thick purée. Cool slightly for 10 minutes.

Preheat the oven to 325°F (160°C, gas mark 3). Butter four 200 ml ramekins, or failing that, a 1 liter terrine. Beat the eggs, add to the pumpkin, blend in food processor, and correct the seasoning as needed. Add half the apple to the pumpkin. Reserve the other half, coated in lemon juice, for decoration.

Place the filled ramekins in a baking dish and pour boiling water around them, then bake for 30 to 45 minutes. The flan should not dry out, or harden, and the blade of knife should come out moist, but clean. Remove from oven and leave to rest for 10 minutes. In the meantime, make the vinaigrette with salt, pepper, vinegar and the two oils. Unmold the flan onto a plate, pour on vinaigrette, arrange the diced apple in a line around the flan and sprinkle with hazelnuts. When the weather turns dreary and cold, this dish is delicate and stunning.

Accompany with a white Cassis.

BOULETTES D'EPINARDS AU BROCCIO

Spinach Croquettes with Broccio (Jean-Jacques Raffiani, Paris Main d'Or)

1 portion Tomato Sauce (see page 42)
1 lb (500 g) spinach
2 eggs
$^1/_2$ cup (75 g) all-purpose (plain) flour
1 lb (500 g) Broccio or Brousse, or even well-
   drained Fromage Blanc, made from ewe's
   milk if possible
$^1/_2$ cup (50 g) freshly grated parmesan
Nutmeg
Salt
Freshly ground pepper

Start with the Tomato Sauce, which can be made in advance (see page 41).

Shortly before mealtime, trim the spinach. Take a leaf in one hand, fold it inward along the stalk, then pull the stem off. It sounds like a complicated operation, but it quickly becomes second nature. Wash and dry the leaves carefully, then wilt the leaves in a pan over high heat, drain again, and squeeze the leaves between your hands to remove any remaining water. Chop coarsely.

In a mixing bowl, beat the eggs with a fork, add the flour, the Broccio, the spinach, 1 tablespoon of the parmesan, and season with nutmeg, salt, and pepper. Mix thoroughly. With your hands, form croquettes the size of a small egg, arrange on a platter and chill in freezer for 10 minutes to make them easier to handle.

In a wide saucepan, bring a large quantity of salted water to a simmer. Drop in the croquettes, and remove with a slotted spoon as soon as they rise to the surface; drain on paper towels. Be careful that the water does not boil or the croquettes will fall apart.

Place a layer of tomato sauce at the bottom of a shallow baking dish , arrange the croquettes on top, sprinkle with parmesan and broil (grill) until golden.

This is a hearty appetizer. It can also be served with a little salad to make a light main course. Accompany with a white Cassis.

ROTIES DE SARDINES ET LEUR TARTARE DE TOMATES

Roast Sardines with a Tomato Tartar (Philippe Tredgeu, Chez Casimir)

4 large, ripe tomatoes, firm and fragrant
2 shallots, preferably the long Jersey type,
    peeled and finely chopped
1 tablespoon chopped flat-leaf parsley or
    chives, chopped
1 tablespoon aged sherry wine vinegar
Sea salt (or even better *fleur de sel* sea salt)
Finely and coarsely ground pepper
2 tablespoons olive oil
12 large sardines, shiny-eyed and firm-fleshed;
    have your fishmonger scale and fillet them
1 small handful of salad greens, for color
    rather than taste, washed and dried
4 slices sourdough bread, crusty outside, dense
    and elastic inside
1 tablespoon balsamic vinegar

Basil Oil
1 bunch basil
1 cup (250 ml) rich-flavored olive oil

Four days before making this dish, prepare the basil oil. On the day of the meal, i.e. on the third night of infusion, strain the basil oil, reserving the chopped basil leaves to be used to make the potatoes on page 76, for example. Both leaves and oil may be kept separately, covered and chilled, for a week.

Half an hour before serving, peel and seed the tomatoes, and cut into small cubes over a bowl. Add the shallots, chopped parsley (or chives), sherry vinegar, and salt and pepper to taste. Mix well.

Preheat oven to 500°F (250°C, gas mark 10). Brush a baking sheet with oil, place the fillets skin side up, brush with more oil, and add salt and pepper. Arrange the salad greens on four plates. Toast the bread until golden. Then place the sardines in the hot oven for 2 minutes until firm.

Place a toasted slice of bread over the greens, garnish with the tomato mixture, remove the fillets with a spatula and arrange them, fanned out, over the top. They are more attractive skin side up. Pour 1 tablespoon of basil oil onto each plate, then sprinkle with a few drops of balsamic vinegar to obtain a stunning marbled effect. Add a pinch of salt, a pinch of coarsely ground pepper, and serve immediately.

TARTARE DE DORADE & NOIX DE SAINT-JACQUES

Dorade Tartare with Dill (Thierry Colas, Marty) &
Scallops with Citrus Vinaigrette (Joël Renty, Brasserie Mollard)

DORADE TARTARE WITH DILL

1 lb (500 g) dorade or porgy, cleaned, skinned,
   and boned by the fishmonger
I small bunch of dill
Juice of 4–5 limes, depending on their size
2 shallots, peeled and finely chopped
6$\frac{1}{2}$ tablespoons olive oil
6$\frac{1}{2}$ tablespoons peanut oil
Salt
1 tablespoon brine-packed green peppercorns,
   rinsed

Dorade Tartare with Dill; the photograph of Scallops with Citrus Vinaigrette appears on page 4.

The night before, mix the dill stems (keep the leafy part in the refrigerator wrapped in a slightly damp towel or cloth as garnish), lime juice, shallots, both oils, pepper, and a generous pinch of salt. Leave to marinate all night. Process or liquidize, then strain through a chinois, pressing firmly with the back of a spoon to extract every drop of flavor.

On a cutting board, chop the dorade as if you were mincing onions. Transfer to a non-reactive bowl, reserve 3 tablespoons of sauce and add the rest to the fish. Add the dill (again keeping some leaves for decoration). Taste and correct salt, if needed. Put the tartare in four small bowls and chill. To serve, unmold onto plates, drizzle a line of sauce around the tartare and decorate with the reserved dill leaves. Serve with toasted bread and a very cold bandol rosé.

SCALLOPS WITH CITRUS VINAIGRETTE

6$\frac{1}{2}$ (200 g) salad greens, washed and diced
1 lemon
1 orange
1 yellow grapefruit
4 cups (1 liter) boiling water
1 packet court bouillon powder
12 scallops, cleaned by the fishmonger
1 small bunch chives, chopped

Vinaigrette
2 tablespoons balsamic vinegar
Salt and freshly ground pepper
6 tablespoons peanut (groundnut) oil

Divide salad greens equally among four plates. Wash and wipe dry the fruits, remove their skin with a zester over a chinois or colander, pour 4 cups (1 liter) boiling water over them, drain and reserve. Make the vinaigrette by whisking together vinegar, salt, pepper, and oil. Make the court bouillon according to the instructions on the package. When it simmers, drop in the scallops with their coral still attached and cook for 1 $\frac{1}{2}$ to 2 minutes. Do not allow them to boil or the flesh will become rubbery. Drain, cut in two, then place the warm scallops on the beds of greens, sprinkle with zests, season with vinaigrette and garnish with chopped chives. Serve this marvelous salad with a gros-plant or a muscadet-sur-lie.

GRATIN D'ECREVISSES

Crayfish Gratin (Patrick Rayer, La Rôtisserie du Beaujolais)

5 shallots, peeled and chopped
$1^1/_4$ tablespoons butter
4 lb (2 kg) crayfish (if unavailable, substitute
   with jumbo shrimp)
$1^1/_2$ cups (400 ml) white dry wine (a Mâcon
   would be perfect)
Rock salt
Table salt
Finely and coarsely ground pepper
$1^1/_4$ cups (300 ml) heavy (double) cream
4 egg yolks
$^1/_2$ cup (50 g) freshly, finely grated
   emmenthal cheese

An hour before mealtime, peel and chop 2 of the shallots, sauté them in butter over low heat, then add the crayfish, half of the wine, a pinch of rock salt and a pinch of coarse pepper and cook for 7 to 8 minutes until the shellfish turn red. Remove with a slotted spoon, place in a dish and allow to cool slightly.

Use this time to chop the remaining shallots, then pour them into a saucepan with the remaining wine, and the strained cooking juice from the crayfish. Reduce by two-thirds over medium heat. Don't fall asleep on the job. By now, the crayfish will have cooled sufficiently to be peeled. Set aside the tails and use the heads for another dish, like a *bisque*.

You now have a third of the juices left in the pan. Add the cream and reduce again, stirring often with a wooden spoon, until the spoon is coated with sauce that is as thick and smooth as custard. Remove the pan from the heat and cool for a few minutes. If there are still a few crayfish to peel, it's now or never.

Light the broiler (grill). In a bowl, whisk the yolks with two or three spoonfuls of sauce then slowly pour the contents of the bowl back into the saucepan, whisking constantly. Taste and correct seasoning if necessary.

Divide the crayfish equally among four individual gratin dishes, or if you do not have any, place in one large baking dish. Cover with sauce, sprinkle with cheese, and brown quickly in the oven for a few seconds.

Enjoy this masterpiece of Burgundian tradition immediately, and accompany with a white Mâcon.

CREVETTES DOREES, ARTICHAUTS ET CELERI AUX AGRUMES

Golden Prawns, Artichokes and Celery with Citrus Fruit (Thierry Colas, Marty)

Scant ¹⁄₂ cup (100 ml) olive oil
1 bunch celery, outer stalks discarded, washed
1 teaspoon coriander seeds or 1 small bunch of
    fresh cilantro (coriander)
Zest of ¹⁄₂ orange
Juice of 2 oranges
Juice of 1 lemon
Salt
Freshly ground pepper
24 large raw shrimp (prawns), peeled

Drain artichoke hearts and pat dry; slice the into thin wedges, like pieces of a pie.

Heat half of the oil in a deep skillet over medium heat and sauté the celery, artichokes, and coriander seeds (if using fresh cilantro add to the pan just before plating) for 5 minutes, stirring from time to time. Add both juices and the zest, salt, and pepper, and cook 10 to 15 minutes until the juice becomes slightly syrupy.

When the vegetables are almost ready, fry the shrimp in a second pan in the remaining oil, over high heat, for 3 or 4 minutes, depending on their size.

Arrange the vegetables on plates, top with the shrimp and serve immediately, accompanied by a white Bandol.

Helpful hints: Substitute 1 small celery root (celeriac) for the celery. Peel and wash it then dice it into ¹⁄₂ -in (1-cm) cubes. For added luxury, cook this dish with raw langoustines (or Dublin Bay prawns).

SARDINES FARCIES AU BROCCIO

Broccio-stuffed Sardines (Jean-Jacques Raffiani, Paris Main d'Or)

3 tablespoons olive oil

13 oz (400 g) baby leeks (white part only),
outer layers and roots discarded, thinly
sliced to yield 6$\frac{1}{2}$ oz (200 g)

1 lb (500 g) Broccio or well-drained *Fromage
Frais*, see Helpful hint

16 plump sardines, scaled and cut into fillets
by a fishmonger

Salt

Freshly ground pepper

Lemon wedges

Preheat the oven to 425°F (220°C, gas mark 7).
Heat 1 tablespoon of the oil over medium heat and
sauté the leek, stirring often to keep it from
browning, which will make it tough. Remove
from heat and transfer to a mizing bowl. Add the
Broccio and mix together with a fork. Add seasoning and stir again.

Oil a baking dish with a further 1 tablespoon of
the oil, insert half the fillets, cover with the leek and
broccoi mixture then add the remaining fillets.
Drizzle with the remaining oil and place in the oven
for 10 minutes. Serve piping hot, with lemon
wedges and a green salad, and accompany with a
Corsican white.

Helpful hint: To make your own fromage frais,
pour 8 cups (2 liters) whole milk (preferably
unpasteurized) into a large saucepan with 4 tablespoons white vinegar and a generous pinch of salt.
Leave over low heat until the mixture curdles in
a pale yellow liquid. Line your chinois or sieve
with a cheesecloth or other very thin fabric, and
pour in the contents of the saucepan. When the
whey has drained completely, you will have a
compact, delicious fromage frais, that you will need
to cool before using. Alternatively, use ewe's milk
as a substitute to fromage frais.

ROUGET A LA TAPENADE, FENOUIL MARINE ET BEURRE BLANC

Mullet with Tapenade, Marinated Fennel, and Beurre Blanc
(Christian Etchebest, Le Troquet)

2 ripe firm tomatoes
6 tablespoons olive oil
2 plump white fennel bulbs
4 red mullets or red gurnards, 6$\frac{1}{2}$ oz (200 g) each, filleted
Juice of 1 lemon
Rock salt and table salt
Freshly ground pepper
1 portion Beurre Blanc (see page 42)

Tapenade
1 oz (30 g) salt-packed anchovies
3$\frac{1}{2}$ oz (100 g) black olives
1 clove garlic
1 teaspoon breadcrumbs
4 tablespoons olive oil

Preheat oven to 150°F (70°C). Peel the tomatoes (see page 33), quarter them, discard the seeds and core, and place the eight "petals" on a baking sheet. Season with salt, pepper, and 2 tablespoons of the oil and bake for 1 hour. Remove and set aside at room temperature.

While the tomatoes are baking, make the tapenade by mixing all the ingredients (see page 52). Process or pound to a paste and set aside.

Remove the stems and the tough, stringy outer leaves of the fennel, then hollow out the core with the tip of a vegetable peeler and discard. Cut the bulbs in half, wash and wipe dry. Slice as thinly as possible, perpendicular to the grain with the cut side down. Transfer to a salad bowl. In a separate bowl, wet a large pinch of rock salt and the same amount of pepper with the juice of 1 lemon. Then add 3 tablespoons of the oil while whisking with a fork and pour this emulsion over the fennel. Mix then set aside to marinate.

Prepare the Beurre Blanc (see page 42).

Season the fillets and cook in a non-stick pan over high heat for 3 minutes, skin side down, with the remaining 1 tablespoon of oil. Place two fillets, skin up oin a plate, garnish the skin with a line of tapenade, place a small mound of marinated fennel in the middle, surround with a little lemon scented *beurre blanc* and finish with 2 tomato petals.

Accompany with a dry Jurançon.

ROUGETS ET CHIPIRONS, FINE RATATOUILLE

Red Mullet and Squid, Served with Delicate Ratatouille
(Jean-Jacques Raffiani, Paris Main d'Or)

1 lb (500 g) squid (the Basque call them *chipiron*)
2 tablespoons olive oil
4 small mullets, scaled and filleted by a fish-monger, seasoned with salt and pepper
4 sprigs fresh rosemary or thyme, to garnish

Ratatouille

2 tablespoons olive oil
1 sprig thyme
1 bay leaf
1 large yellow onion, peeled and chopped
2 cloves garlic, peeled and chopped
1 red bell pepper (capsicum), cut into long strips
1 eggplant (aubergine), cut into thick batons
2 zucchini (courgettes), cut into thick batons
4 plump tomatoes, peeled, seeded, and coarsley chopped

Vinaigrette

Juice of 1 lemon
Salt
Freshly ground pepper
4 tablespoons olive oil

One hour in advance, start cooking the ratatouille. In a large pan, heat the oil, thyme, and bay leaf over medium heat, then add onion and garlic. Add the bell pepper, eggplant, zucchini, and tomatoes, waiting for each vegetable to soften slightly before adding the next. Do not let your wooden spoon rest, the vegetables should not brown! Cook 30 to 40 minutes, stirring from time to time, until the mixture thickens. Discard thyme and bay leaves before plating.

Make the vinaigrette dressing by whisking together the lemon juice, salt, pepper, and oil. Set aside.

While the ratatoille is still cooking, clean the squid. Cut off and discard the eyes and head, detach, wash and drain the ring the tentacles, cutting out the tough center. Slice open the body and discard everything it contains under cold running water and rub off the thin outer film that comes off easily. Drain.

When the vegetables are nearly ready, heat 2 tablespoons oil in a large non-stick pan and add the squid and fish (skin side down); cook for 4 minutes, stirring the squid occasionally, then turn the mullet over, and cook for 1 more minute. Plate the ratatouille, then place two fillets skin side up on each plate, surrounded by a circle of squid. Garnish with a sprig of fresh rosemary or thyme. You will just about be able to hear the chirping cicadas, as you do in Provence. Accompany with a white Cassis.

FILETS DE DORADE ROTIS,
POMMES DE TERRE AU BASILIC

Roast Fillest of Dorade with Basil Potatoes (Philippe Tredgeu, Chez Casimir)

2 lb (1 kg) firm potatoes (such as BF 15, roseval, or charlotte), washed and patted dry
$^{1}/_{3}$ cup (60 g) butter, plus a little for the pan
Bunch fresh basil, chopped
Salt and *fleur de sel* (sea salt crystals)
1 tablespoon olive oil
4 dorades or porgies, 10–16 oz (300–500 g) each, scaled and filleted with skin intact
Mignonnette (coarsely ground pepper)
Few stalks dill, to garnish
4 tablespoons basil oil (see page 58), strained or unstrained, mixed with 1 tablespoon balsamic vinegar, to garnish

One and a half hours before the meal, preheat the oven to 360° F (180°C, gas mark 4). Wrap each potato in aluminum foil, place on a rack in the middle of the oven and bake for 1 hour. When the hour is up, test for doneness by inserting the tip of a knife, which should meet with no resistance. If this is not the case, leave them a little longer. Discard the foil, peel, then transfer to a bowl with butter, basil, and salt. Mash the potatoes with a fork and keep warm.

Place a non-stick pan containing the oil and a little butter over medium heat. When the butter foams, raise the heat slightly, place the fillets skin side down and cook for 3 to 5 minutes depending on their size, then flip over for a few seconds more.

Place a circle of potato in the center of each plate, place two fillets on top, sprinkle with a little fleur de sel, a pinch of *mignonette*, and decorate with a sprig of dill. Garnish with a ring of basil oil mixed with a few drops of balsamic vinegar. Serve this robust, savory dish immediately, and accompany with a bottle of Touraine or saumur.

SOLE MEUNIERE, POMMES VAPEUR

Sole Meuniere with Steamed Potatoes (Joël Renty, Brasserie Mollard)

8 potatoes that remain firm when cooked (such as charlottes or BF 15), peeled, washed and patted dry

Salt

4 single serving soles, skinned on the black side and scraped clean on the white side

Freshly ground pepper

Scant $^1/_2$ cup (50 g) flour

1 tablespoon peanut (groundnut) oil

$^1/_2$ cup (100 g) butter

2 lemons, cut in wedges

Sprinkle the potatoes with salt, and steam for about 20 minutes (test for doneness with the tip of a knife).

After cooking the potatoes for 10 minutes start the fish. Season the sole with salt and pepper, place the flour in a plate then flour the fish lightly, shaking off any excess. In a large non-stick pan, heat the oil and a lump of the butter (not all the butter) and cook the fish, 4 minutes each side.

Meanwhile, melt the rest of the butter in a small saucepan until it foams and reaches a deep golden color (but don't let it burn!). This is noisette butter, which will be used as a sauce.

When the fish is cooked, sprinkle on a few drops of lemon juice, place on heated plates, cover with a little noisette butter, garnish with potatoes and lemon wedges and serve immediately. It is hard to be any more Parisian than this brasserie classic. Accompany with a Riesling or muscadet-sur-lie.

DOS DE LOUP GRILLE, ARTICHAUTS EN BARIGOULE

Grilled Bass with "Barigoule" Artichokes (Flora Mikula, Les Olivades)

Barigoule usually refers to stewed artichokes. Here they are served mixed with their garnish.

8 small globe artichokes
$\frac{1}{3}$ cups (100 ml) olive oil + 1 tablespoon to oil the roasting griddle
2 carrots, peeled, washed and diced
3 shallots, peeled and chopped
3 cloves garlic, peeled and chopped
1 teaspoon coriander seeds
Juice of 1 lemon
3 sprigs thyme
2 bay leaves
2 cups (500 ml) white wine
Salt
Freshly ground pepper
2-4 lb (1–2 kg) sea bass or bar, filleted, each fillet cut into 4 equal slices, leaving the skin on
10 oz (300 g) fava (broad) beans, peeled and blanched 2 minutes, refreshed in cold water and white covering removed (see page 46)
1 preserved lemon in brine, chopped
1 small bunch fresh cilantro (coriander), roughly chopped
About 20 small black olives, preferably from Nice, to garnish

Cilantro oil

1 small bunch fresh cilantro (coriander) leaves
$\frac{3}{4}$ cup (200 ml) olive oil
large pinch salt

Make cilantro oil by processing the cilantro leaves, oil, and salt. Set aside to be used as a sauce.

Remove the tough outer leaves from the artichoke. Trim all but one-quarter of the stem, cut each artichoke in half, remove the fuzz, and trim the tops of the leaves. Pour $\frac{1}{3}$ cup (100 ml) of oil into a wide, deep saucepan, and, over medium heat, sauté the carrots, shallots and garlic, stirring from time to time. Then add the artichokes, coriander seeds, lemon juice, thyme, bay leaves, and wine. Add salt and pepper, and cook over low heat for 20 minutes, until the artichoke are tender but still have some bite. When the artichokes are ready, add the beans to the pan, together with the preserved lemon and cilantro. Bring to a boil before serving, and taste and correct seasoning as needed.

Meanwhile, preheat the oven to 410°F (210°C, gas mark 6½). Place the slices of bass on an oiled non-stick roasting griddle or tray, skin side down, and bake in the oven for 10 to 15 minutes.

Arrange the reheated vegetables on each plate, place the bass in the middle, season with salt and pepper and a drizzle of cilantro oil, garnish with olives and serve immediately. Accompany with a white Châteauneuf-du-pape.

STEAK DE THON AU BEURRE D'ORANGE, POÊLEE DE COURGETTES

Tuna Steaks with Orange Butter and Zucchini Garnish
(Stéphane Baron, Le Zéphyr)

1 portion Orange Buerre Blanc Sauce (see page 42)
1 tablespoon butter
3 tablespoons olive oil
2 lb (1 kg) small, firm zucchini (courgettes), tipes trimmed, slice into thin rounds or dice
Salt
Freshly ground pepper
1 sprig fresh (or dried) rosemary
4 small, thick tuna steaks, about 6$\frac{1}{2}$ oz (200 g) each, at room temperature (substitute with bonito or swordfish)
Cherry tomatoes, to garnish (optional)

Firstly, prepare the Orange Buerre Blanc Sauce (see page 42) and keep warm until ready to serve.

In a large pan, heat 1 tablespoon butter and 2 tablespoons of the oil, then stir in the zucchini until it is cooked but still crisp. Season with salt, pepper, and a few needles of rosemary.

When the zucchini is almost done, turn your attention to the tuna. Sear one side in a very hot non-stick pan containing the remaining oil; turn over as soon as it has browned, after about 1 minute, lower the heat, cover and cook for a further 4 minutes. Season with salt and pepper.

Place zucchini in the center of each plate, top with tuna, pour the butter over the tuna, and serve immediately. Cherry tomatoes can be added for a nice touch of color. Accompany with a white Graves or a Chardonnay

TOURNEDOS DE SAUMON AU JAMBON, SAUCE VIERGE

Ham-wrapped Salmon Tournedos with Sauce Vierge
(Christian Etchebest, Le Troquet)

4 large, thin slices of Bayonne ham (substitute with *prosciutto* or other dry ham)
1 lb 3 oz (600 g) fillet of salmon, skinned and boned
1 portion Sauce Vierge (see page 42)
2 fennel bulbs
4 tablespoons olive oil
2 carrots, peeled, washed and cut into rounds
2 turnips, peeled, washed and cut into rounds
2 zucchini (courgettes), washed and cut into rounds
1 sprig thyme
1 bay leaf
Salt
Freshly ground pepper

One hour before the meal, place the slices of ham on a piece of waxed (greaseproof) paper, overlapping slightly. Place the salmon on top, perpendicular to the ham, roll into a sausage lengthwise, using the paper to push it along, and seal the roll tightly. Place in the refrigerator, where the whole thing will meld.

Next make the Sauce Vierge and set aside at room temperature until ready to serve.

Discard the stems and the outer layers of the fennel, cut off the core with the tip of a peeler or paring knife in a cone shape, split each bulb in two from top to bottom, then slice thickly, in the same direction. Pour 2 tablespoons of the oil into a wide saucepan, sauté first the carrots, then at 3 minute intervals, add the turnips, then the fennel, and finally the zucchini. Add the thyme and bay leaf, and leave to simmer for 15 minutes, stirring from time to time.

While the vegetables are simmering, remove the fish from the refrigerator. Remove it from its paper, and slice the sausage into four equal pieces. Heat a non-stick pan with the remaining oil, and cook the tournedos for 5 minutes on each side.

Warm the sauce over low heat. While the sauce is warming, garnish the plates with the vegetables, place a tournedos on top, and cover each one with 2 tablespoons of sauce. This version of surf and turf will send you soaring. Accompany this dish with a white Irouleguy.

CROUSTILLANT DE BARBUE, SAUCE CHAMPAGNE

Crispy Brill and Champagne Sauce (Catherine Guerraz, Chez Catherine)

3 medium carrots, peeled, cut in short lengths
3 small zucchini (courgettes), tips trimmed, cut in short lengths
4 miniature patty pans or other baby squash
1 portion Champagne Sauce (see page 42)
2 lb (1 kg) brill, scaled and cut into 4 equal fillets (substitute with turbot)
Salt
Freshly ground pepper
Coriander seeds
Fennel seeds
4 sheets phyllo pastry
1 egg yolk
2 tablespoons olive oil

Salad

Selection of dill, chervil, flat leaf parsley, and tarragon leaves
1 tablespoon olive oil

Prepare the vegetables in advance. Boil the carrots in salted water for five minutes, add the zucchini and patty pans and cook for 5 minutes more. The vegetables must remain firm. Drain, plunge into iced water, drain again, and reserve. When you are ready to serve, reheat them in a double boiler or microwave.

Prepare the Champagne Sauce (see page 42) and keep warm until ready to serve.

Preheat oven to 475°F (240°C, gas mark 9). Sprinkle each piece of brill with salt, pepper, a good pinch of coriander and fennel and place on a sheet of pastry. Fold the pastry as if you were wrapping a package, and brush egg yolk over the edges to seal. In a pan over high heat, sear both sides of the packets in 2 tablespoons of the oil. Transfer to a baking tray and bake in the oven for another 10 minutes.

To make the salad, toss the leaves with a pinch of salt and the oil. To assemble, pour a small ladleful of sauce onto each plate, place a packet topped with salad on the sauce, surround with reheated vegetables, and serve immediately. This dish is as attractive as it is tasty! Accompany with a white Châteauneuf-du-pape.

PAVE DE TURBOT ROTI AUX BLETTES, SAUCE VIN ROUGE

Roast Steaks of Turbot with Swiss Chard and Red Wine Sauce
(André Signoret, Le Train Bleu)

2 lb (1 kg) swiss chard
Juice of 1 lemon
1 tablespoon all-purpose (plain) flour
2 tablespoons olive oil
1 tablespoon rock salt
1 portion Red Wine Sauce (page 43)
$1^3/_4$ tablespoons butter
1 sprig thyme
1 bay leaf
2 cloves garlic, unpeeled
4 Turbot steaks, 8 oz (250 g) each, with skin
  intact, seasoned with salt and pepper
1 large firm potato, peeled, 4 thin slices cut from
  the center (discard the rest of the potato)
1 small bunch chives
A few basil leaves or a few sprigs of chervil

About an hour before serving, carefully wash the swiss chard, separate the leaves from the stalks, chop the leaves (discarding any that are too tough), and set aside. Trim the stalks of their tough outer fibers, and cut into $1^1/_2$-in (4-cm) lengths. In a saucepan, add the lemon juice, the flour dissolved in a little cold water, 1 tablespoon of the oil, 1 tablespoon rock salt, and enough water to cover the stalks. Bring to a boil, add the stalks, boil for 15 minutes. Drain. Set aside.

While the stalks are cooking (this is called *au blanc* in classical French cuisine), prepare the Red Wine Sauce (see page 43). Preheat oven to 360°F (180°C, gas mark 4). In a non-stick, ovenproof pan, heat the remaining 1 tablespoon oil, half of the butter, the thyme, bay leaf, and the unpeeled garlic. Place the four potato slices in the pan and top each slice with a piece of turbot, flesh side down. Cook gently for 10 minutes over medium heat, then transfer to the oven and bake for a further 10 minutes.

While the fish is baking, reheat the stalks and greens in the remaining butter over high heat, stirring often. Remove from heat and add 2 tablespoons chopped chives, basil or chervil.Serve the turbot steaks, with the potato on top, in the middle of the plate, flanked on one side with chard, and on the other with sauce. Accompany with a red Bouzy or Sancerre.

CABILLAUD AUX EPICES, EPINARDS AU BASILIC

Spiced Cod with Spinach and Basil (Tsukasa Fukuyama, A & M Le Bistrot)

2 lb (1 kg) spinach, preferably small leaves
$^1/_3$ cup (100 ml) veal fond
Spice mixture comprising 1 tablespoon ground
    cinnamon, $^1/_2$ tablespoon Madras (medium
    hot) curry powder, and $^1/_4$ tablespoon celery
    salt
4 cod steaks, about 5 oz (160 g) each, skin intact
    or removed
6 tablespoons olive oil
1 lump butter
A dozen or so basil leaves, shredded by hand
Rock salt and table salt
Mignonette peppercorns and freshly ground
    pepper
1 small bunch chives

Trim and carefully wash and dry the spinach (see page 56) in advance. Everything else can be done in a flash, just before serving.

To make the sauce, heat the veal fond and a small pinch of the spice mixture, and reduce by half over low heat. Set aside.

Coat one side (the flesh side if you have kept the skin) of the cod with the remaining spice mixture and add a few grinds of pepper. Pour half the oil into a non-stick pan and cook the cod over high heat, 2 minutes spice side down, then 4 minutes on the other side.

Meanwhile, over medium heat, heat the butter in a wide saucepan until it turns deep gold (this is noisette butter). Toss the spinach in the butter and cook until all the water it releases has evaporated. Season with salt and pepper, and mix in the basil leaves.

Garnish each plate with spinach, place a cod steak, spice side up, on the spinach and surround with sauce. Drizzle the remaining oil over the sauce, in droplets like pearls, add a pinch of *mignonette*, a line of rock salt, and another of chives. Enjoy! Accompany with a white Beaujolais or a Côteax-d'Aix vieilles vignes.

PAVE DE CABILLAUD ROTI A L'AIL DOUX ET SON GRATIN

Roast Cod with Sweet Garlic and Gratin
(Patrick Rayer, La Rôtisserie du Beaujolais)

3 bulbs garlic
8 oz (250 g) goose fat or 1 cup (250 ml) peanut (groundnut) oil
4 cod steaks, $6^1/_2$ oz (200 g) each, with skin intact, seasoned with salt and pepper
4 slightly floury potatoes (such as bintjes), peeled, washed and wiped, very thinly sliced using a mandolin
6 tablespoons butter
1 chicken bouillon cube
$3/_4$ cup (200 ml) water
2 tablespoons olive oil
Salt
Freshly ground pepper

Start with the garlic, which must be prepared in advance (a day before serving, if possible). Open the bulbs of garlic, delicately separating the cloves without detaching them from the base. Place in a snuggly fitted saucepan, cover with goose fat or oil, and cook over low heat for 30 minutes. The fat should barely simmer. Any hotter, and your sweet garlic will become charred garlic. Leave to cool in the saucepan at room temperature for up to 24 hours.

Meanwhile, make the stock with the chicken bouillon cube and $3/_4$ cup (200 ml) water. Set aside.

Preheat oven to 400°F (200°C, gas mark 6). Butter 4 individual baking dishes with 2 tablespoons butter, sprinkle with salt and pepper, then add the potato slices in layers like the petals of a daisy, largely overlapping in a single layer, finishing with the last slice at the center of the "flower." Season again, scatter another 2 tablespoons butter (cut into small pieces), and bake until golden brown, about 10 to 15 minutes.

Brush a non-stick baking tray with olive oil, and place the cod on the tray, skin side down. When the potatoes are just about done, place the tray of cod over a high flame for 2 minutes. Remove the potatoes from the oven, and place the cod in the center of the oven, turning the temperature up to maximum and roasting for 10 minutes.

When the cod steaks are done, transfer them to a dish and keep warm, together with the potato gratins, in the oven, switched off with the door propped open. Pour the stock into the roasting pan to deglaze, scraping gently with a spatula, and reduce by half over high heat. Off the heat, add the remaining 2 tablespoons butter, cut into chunks, with a whisk.

Now take the garlic out of the fat in which it has been resting, and reheat for 3 minutes in a microwave. Alternatively, reheat gently in the oil, then drain. These aromatic garlic cloves will be used as garnish. To assemble, unmold the gratins in the middle of each plate, place a steak, skin side up on the gratins, pour a ring of sauce around and garnish with garlic cloves. Accompany with a Chablis or a Saint-Véran.

GALETTES DE BRANDADE DE MORUE, COMPOTEE DE TOMATES

Salt Cod Fishcakes with Tomato Compote (Flora Mikula, Les Olivades)

Salt cod requires pre-soaking, so you must start preparing this recipe two days in advance.

- 2 lb (1 kg) salt cod, cut into pieces
- 3 medium potatoes (such as bintjes), peeled, washed and cut into thin slices
- 2 bouquets garnis (each made of 3 stalks parsley, 1 sprig thyme, and 1 bay leaf)
- 1 plump bulb garlic, split in two, one half left whole, one half separated into cloves, peeled, finely chop 5 cloves and thinly slice 3 cloves (keep separate)
- $3/_4$ cup (200 ml) olive oil, plus 2 tablespoons extra
- $3/_4$ cup (200 ml) heavy (double) cream
- 1 onion, peeled and thinly sliced
- 2 lb (1 kg) tomatoes on the vine, peeled, seeded and chopped
- 1 tablespoon sugar
- 2 tablespoons black olives, from Nice if you can get them, pitted and chopped
- Salt
- Freshly ground pepper

Salad

- Assorted chervil, tarragon, and dill leaves
- Juice of 1 lemon
- 2 tablspoons olive oil

Two days before serving, soak the salt cod in cold water, changing the water frequently. Remove the skin and bones (which is very easy after soaking). On the day of the meal, place potatoes in a stockpot with the cod, 1 bouquet garni, and half the garlic bulb. Cover with cold water, bring to a simmer, and poach for 15 minutes, without any boiling whatsoever. Drain the stockpot, discarding the bouquet garni and garlic. Check the cod for any remaining bones, then shred the fish into a food processor, and add the potatoes.

Get two small saucepans ready on the oven. In one pan place chopped garlic and $3/_4$ cup olive oil; in the other pan pour the cream. Heat both pans and, as soon as they boil, switch on the processor, and add the oil and the cream a little at a time, alternating between the two. The mixture should be thick but creamy. Correct seasoning with salt and pepper, then set aside. Sauté sliced garlic and onion in 1 tablespoon of oil, then add tomatoes (see page 33), 1 bouquet garni, sugar, and salt to taste. Cook for 30 mins over medium heat, stirring from time to time, then add the olives.

Meanwhile, prepare a salad by combining leaves, salt, pepper and lemon juice, and 2 tablespoons olive oil. When the tomato compote in done, take the cod mixture and shape into 8 thick patties. Brown them in remaining 1 tablespoon of oil on both sides, but don't rush things. To assemble, garnish each plate with tomato compote, top with fishcakes, and surround with a ring of salad. Accompany with a Bandol rosé.

SUPREME DE VOLAILLE EN CROUTE DE NOIX AU ROMARIN

Chicken Breasts in a Walnut and Rosemary Crust
(Tsukasa Fukuyama, A & M Le Bistrot)

4 free-range chicken breasts, with skin
Salt
Freshly ground pepper
Scant $^1/_2$ cup (50 g) all-purpose (plain) flour
$^1/_3$ cup (100 ml) peanut oil
$^1/_2$ cup (100 g) butter
$^1/_3$ cup (40 g) chopped walnuts
8 sprigs rosemary, chopped

Side vegetables
2 bunches of asparagus
$1^1/_2$ tablespoons butter
Salt

First prepare the side vegetables. If using asparagus (see Helpful hint for alternative side vegetables), discard the tough end of the stalk, cut into pieces and boil in salted water for 3 to 5 minutes, depending on size. Drain, plunge in iced water, and drain again. When you are ready to serve, toss them in hot butter over low heat.

Rub the chicken breasts with salt and pepper, then coat in flour, shaking off any excess. In a skillet, heat oil and half of the butter over medium heat until the mixture foams. Add chicken and cook 5 minutes, skin side down, until golden, then turn over and cook a further 3 minutes. Cover, remove from heat and set aside 5 minutes.

Prepare noisette butter (see page 74) using the remaining butter. Reheat the vegetables.

Place a drained breast on each plate, sprinkle with walnuts and a couple of pinches of rosemary, pour on a drizzle of noisette butter, and garnish with a side vegetable of your choice. Accompany with a white Burgundy.

Helpful hints: An alternative side vegetable to the asparagus is cabbage and juniper berries. Discard the tough outer leaves of 1 green cabbage, delicately remove the inner leaves from the tender heart and blanche them in a large quantity of water salted with rock salt for about 3 minutes. Drain thoroughly. Before serving, make a noisette butter (see page 78) from 1/4 cup (50 g) butter, then reheat the cabbage in it and season with 1 tablespoon crushed juniper berries.

MAGRET DE CANARD, POINTES D'ASPERGES AU JUS

Duck Breast and Asparagus Tips (Benoît Chagny, A & M Le Bistrot)

2 bunches of medium-sized green asparagus,
   tough stalk ends discarded, trimmed to the
   same length
2 duck breasts, preferably from fattened ducks
   from southwest France
Quatre-épices (a classical spice mix, usually a
   blend of nutmeg, ginger, cloves, and white
   pepper)
1 teaspoon peanut oil
$^1/_3$ cup (100 ml) veal fond
$1^1/_2$ tablespoons butter
$^1/_3$ cup (30 g) parmesan
Rock salt and table salt
Pepper

Boil asparagus in water that has been generously salted with rock salt for about 5 minutes. Test for doneness by pricking the thickest part of a stalk with a toothpick. It should enter easily and the texture should be both firm and tender. Cool asparagus under running water, pat dry and cut in half. Set aside.

Using the tip of a small paring knife, remove the troublesome nerve that runs the length of the breast, then score the skin making diamond shapes. Rub the flesh with quatre-épices, salt, and pepper. Rub the surface of a heavy pan with oil, place over medium heat, and place the breasts skin side down. The breasts will render sufficient fat. Keep spooning the melted fat over the meat (the French say you are "feeding" the meat.) When the skin becomes crisp (about 10 minutes), add 3 tablespoons boiling water, turn the breasts over, and cook briefly. Remove from pan and drain on a wire rack and allow the meat to rest for as long as it cooked: a further 10 minutes. Doing so will ensure that the duck is incredibly tender.

Heat a broiler (grill). Discard all but 3 tablespoons fat from the pan. Add the veal fond, and gently detach the cooked-on juices at the bottom of the pan and reduce until slightly syrupy, season with salt and pepper and strain through a chinois or sieve into a small saucepan. Add half the butter, whisk and hold over the lowest heat possible.

In another pan, roll the asparagus in the rest of the butter and reheat, but do not allow to color. Add 1 tablespoon of sauce and roll again.

Slice the duck breasts and fan out on 4 dinner plates, place under the broiler for 30 seconds to warm through, garnish with the asparagus, either criss-crossed or in a circle around the meat, top with a little sauce, add a few strips of parmesan, and serve. Accompany with a Madivan or Cahors.

CANARD ROTI, LEGUMES NOUVEAUX

Roast Duck with Baby Vegetables (Patrick Rayer, La Rôtisserie du Beaujolais)

2 quarts (2 liters) water with a generous pinch of rock salt
10 oz (300 g) snow peas (*mange-tout*), trimmed
10 oz (300 g) very slender French beans, trimmed
10 oz (300 g) small new turnips, peeled (leaving a little green stem)
10 oz (300 g) small new carrots, peeled (leaving a little green stem)
1 duck, about 5 lb (2$^1/_2$ kg), with its offal roughly chopped
2 large carrots, diced
2 large onions, peeled and diced
1 head of garlic, cut in half
1 chicken bouillon cube
2 cups (500 ml) boiling water
2 tablespoons butter
Rock salt and table salt
Mignonnette (coarsely cracked pepper) and freshly ground pepper

At least 2 hours before mealtime, prepare the vegetables. Bring salted water to a boil, and cook the vegetables separately in the following order: snow peas, for 3 minutes after the water returns to a boil; green beans, 5 minutes; turnips, 7 minutes; carrots, 10 minutes. Strain with a slotted spoon, refresh under cold running water and reserve separately.

Preheat oven to 425°F (220°C, gas mark 7). Rub the duck inside and out with rock salt and *mignonnette*, place in a roasting pan, and place in the middle of the oven for 15 minutes. Reduce heat to 400°F (200°C, gas mark 6) and bake for 10 minutes. Add the roughly chopped offal and bake for a further 10 minutes, then add carrot, onion, and garlic,a nd continue baking for 15 minutes (the duck will have been in the oven for a total of 50 minutes).

Meanwhile, make a stock with 2 cups (500 ml) boiling water and the chicken bouillon cube.

Remove the duck, place on a dish and cover with aluminum foil. The blood that was forced into the center of the animal will now have time to spread back through the meat, giving it the desired degree of tenderness. Reduce oven temperature to 325°F (160°C, gas mark 3).

Skim off the fat from the roasting pan with a spoon. Add the stock, scrape the cooked on bits with a spatula, and reduce by slightly more than half, to a scant 1 cup (200 ml). This will take about 15 minutes.

In an ovenproof serving platter, arrange the cooled vegetables, and season lightly. With a large sharp knife, split the duck into two halves, along the breast bone, and place on the bed of vegetables. Moisten with the sauce poured through a chinois or sieve, pressing slightly with a spoon to extract all the flavor. Scatter the butter over the top, then place in the oven for 10 minutes to heat through. Accompany with a bottle of Vacqueyras.

PINTADE CONFITE ET HARICOTS VERTS
A LA TAPENADE

Guinea Fowl with Green Beans and Olive Paste (Philippe Tredgeu, Chez Casimir)

4 guinea fowl legs, skin on (substitute with
    4 rabbit legs for Lapin Confit)
4 cups (1 liter) olive oil + 1 tablespoon extra
2 lb (1 kg) green beans
1 lump butter
Pepper from the mill

Marinade

2 lb (1 kg) rock salt
4 sprigs thyme
4 large cloves garlic

Tapenade

5 oz (150 g) black olives
1 clove garlic
1 oz (30 g) anchovies (salt packed)
3 tablespoons olive oil

The day before, arrange the pieces of poultry in a shallow dish in a single layer, place a sprig of thyme and a crushed, unpeeled clove of garlic on each piece. Cover with a layer of rock salt, chill and marinate overnight.

The next day, remove the meat from its marinade and wipe thoroughly with a clean cloth. You will note that the flesh has become slightly firm.

Heat 4 cups oil to 175°F (80°C) in a large shallow saucepan (the oil should barely be simmering). Add the meat and cook for 1 hour over constant low heat. You may need to add an isolating pad between the flame and the pot. All confits require long cooking over low heat.

While the meat is cooking, trim the beans, and cook in a little salted boiling water. Boil for just a few minutes, keeping them a little crisp. Drain and cool under cool running water. Set aside.

Make the tapenade with the olives, garlic, anchovies, a little freshly ground pepper, and 3 tablespoons oil (see page 52). In a blender or food procesor, make a paste that is uniform and firm.

Just before serving, heat 2 tablespoons water, 1 tablespoon oil, and the butter in a saucepan. When it comes to a boil, whisk the mixture to form an emulsion. Add the beans, and cook just long enough to reheat, stirring gently with a wodden spoon. Remove from the heat, add 2 tablespoons of the tapenade and mix well.

Remove the meat from the oil with a slotted spoon and drain on paper towels. Quickly make a bed of vegetables on each plate, top with a piece of meat and serve. This dish is also delicous with green peas, fava beans, or mashed potatoes. Whatever the accompaniment, do not forget the Tapenade. If you have some left over, spread it on toasted bread and enjoy. Accompany with a red Madiran, Cahors, or Béarn.

STEAK TARTARE & FILET DU BOEUF

Steak Tartare (André Signoret, Le Train Bleu) &
Beef Fillet with Potato Gratin (Jöel Renty, Brasserie Mollard)

STEAK TARTARE

1¹/₂ lb (700 g) well-aged fillet of beef
4 egg yolks
4 teaspoons hot mustard
4 teaspoons oil
Dash of Tabasco
Salt
Freshly ground pepper
4 tablespoons finely chopped shallots
4 tablespoons finely chopped pickles (gherkins)
4 tablespoons finely chopped flat leaf parsley
4 tablespoons of capers in vinegar, drained

On a cutting board, finely mince the meat with a sharp knife (an electric meat grinder will only give you mush). Pour into a mixing bowl.

In a bowl, mix the yolks and mustard and add the oil, drop by drop, as if you were making mayonnaise, then season with a dash of Tabasco, and a sprinkling of salt and pepper. Pour over the meat, add the chopped condiments and capers, and mix thoroughly. Serve with a green salad and a slightly chilled Beaujolais.

BEEF FILLET WITH POTATO GRATIN

1 clove garlic
4 thick slices fillet cut beef (see page 39), 6 oz
(180 g) per person, from well-aged beef
2 lb (1 kg) waxy potatoes (such as bintje), peeled, washed and patted dry, thinly sliced
3 cups (750 ml) fresh whole milk
1 egg, beaten
1¹/₄ cups (175 g) grated cheese
Salt
Freshly ground pepper
Nutmeg
1¹/₂ tablespoons butter

Preheat the oven to 360°F (180°C, gas mark 4). Peel the garlic, split the clove and rub it over a shallow earthenware baking dish. Boil the milk and pour over the potatoes in a mixing bowl. Add 4 oz (125 g) of the cheese, the beaten egg, salt, pepper, and grated nutmeg to season. Mix well. Pour the potatoes into the garlicky baking dish, cover with the rest of the grated cheese and scatter with small lumps of butter. Bake for at least 40 minutes until the potatoes are tender and the top golden.

Just before serving, place the steaks in a heavy skillet that has been heated over high heat. Cook for 3 minutes on each side—fillets should always be served a rosy medium rare. Season, then place on warmed plates, an garnish, if you want to respect tradition, with a small bunch of cress. Serve the potato gratin separately. Serve this classical dish with a Saint-Emilion or a red Graves.

DAUBE AU VIN ROUGE

Beef Simmered in Red Wine (Jean-Jacques Raffiani, Paris Main d'Or)

Make your *daube* a day in advance; it is much better reheated.

4 tablespoons olive oil
2 lb (1 kg) beef short ribs, cut into 3 1/2-oz (100-g) piececs
3 large onions, peeled and chopped
4 cloves garlic, peeled and chopped
5 oz (150 g) smoked slab bacon, with its rind, cubed
1 tablespoon all-purpose (plain) flour
4 large, ripe tomatoes, peeled, seeded, and chopped (see page 33)
1 heaping tablespoon of tomato paste (concentrate)
1 bottle Corsican red wine, or failing that, another tannic red wine
1 bouquet garni comprising 4 sprigs parsley, 1 sprig thyme, and 1 bay leaf
Rock salt
Black peppercorns

Pour half the oil into a large cast-iron pot, and heat until it begins to smoke. Brown the meat on all sides. When there is no juice remaining in the pot, remove the meat with a slotted spoon, and lower the heat. Add onions, garlic, and bacon to the pot with the remaining oil, and sauté, stirring from time to time.

When the onions are transparent, put the meat, and its juices, back into the pot, sprinkle with flour and stir thoroughly. Add the tomato and the concentrate, wine, bouquet garni, a little rock salt, 10 peppercorns, and enough water to cove. Stir and bring to a boil. Reduce heat to the minimum and simmer, covered, for 3 hours, or even better, bake in an oven heated to 300°F (150°C, gas mark 2) if the lid is ovenproof (this is not always the case). Cool to room temperature and reserve.

The next day, reheat the stew gently, 30 minutes over low heat, and serve with polenta or large pasta shapes like macaroni. A bottle of Mercurey would make a fine accompaniment.

POT-AU-FEU DANS SA TRADITION

Traditional Pot-Au-Feu (Thierry Colas, Marty)

2 lb (1 kg) stewing beef, using 2 different cuts from the following list: shank, short ribs, flank, or brisket
1 onion, peeled and studded with 1 clove
2 cloves garlic, peeled
1 bouquet garni comprising 4 or 5 sprigs of parsley, 1 sprig thyme, 1 bay leaf
Handful rock salt
10 peppercorns
4 small leeks, washed, most of the green trimmed off
4 turnips, peeled and washed
4 carrots, peeled and washed
4 firm potatoes (such as charlottes), peeled and washed
4 pieces of celery root (celeriac), approximately half a bulb, washed
4 marrow bone pieces, each cut to 2 in (5 cm) in length
Fresh thyme
Pepper
3$\frac{1}{2}$ oz (100 g) vermicelli pasta
Nutmeg

Garnish

Rock salt
Small cornichon pickles or gherkins
Pickled onions
A selection of mustards and horseradish

Four hours before the meal, place the meat in a stock pot with the onion, garlic, bouquet garni, a handful of rock salt, and about 10 peppercorns. Add cold water to cover by 2 in (5 cm), and bring to a boil. Remove the scum that rises to the surface with a slotted spoon, then leave simmering for 3 hours. Add the vegetables and cook for a further 45 minutes.

Preheat oven to 400°F (200°C, gas mark 6). Place the marrow bones in a roasting pan, sprinkle with rock salt and loose leaf thyme, add pepper and set aside.

Just before serving, remove 4 ladlesful of broth to a saucepan (leaving the meat and vegetables to simmer, covered, in the remaining liquid). Bring to a boil, cook the pasta and serve in individual bowls, with a little grated nutmeg if you like (even though Thierry Colas would not approve, but like all questions of taste, this is a very personal matter!). Just before sitting down to enjoy the stock, do not forget to place the marrow bones into the oven for 15 minutes.

Once you have cleared away the bowls, serve the drained vegetables and meats, along with the roasted marrow, on a large platter. Pass around toasted bread for the marrow. Each diner helps him or herself to the garnishes and condiments. Served in this manner, a pauper's dish becomes a dish fit for a king. Accompany with a Morgon or a Juliénas.

HACHIS PARMENTIER

French Shepherd's Pie (Tsukasa Fukuyama, A & M Le Bistrot)

1½ lb (750 g) stewing beef (cheeks, shanks or brisket) or 2 lb (1 kg) oxtail
2 large onions, peeled and chopped
1 carrot, peeled and chopped
1 stalk celery, peeled and chopped
3 cloves garlic, peeled
1 sprig thyme
1 bay leaf
1 clove
1½ lb (750 g) waxy potatoes (such as *bintjes*), peeled and washed
¾ cup (150 g) butter, at room temperature
⅔ cup (150 ml) milk
2 tablespoon peanut (groundnut) oil
1 small bunch flat leaf parsley
Rock salt and table salt
Black peppercorns and pepper from the mill

Place the meat in a stockpot, cover with boiling water, and bring to a boil. Skim the scum that rises to the top as the water boils, then add half the onion, the chopped vegetables, garlic, thyme, bay leaf, clove, and a dozen or so peppercorns. Leave to cook at a low simmer for 3 hours, covered.

About 1 hour before the meat is done, place potatoes in a pot with some rock salt, cover with cold water and bring to a boil. Boil 20 to 30 minutes, until the potatoes can be pierced with the tip of a knife without offering any resistance. Drain, put through a food mill, and transfer to a bowl containing the butter, stir with a wooden spoon but do not overmix (doing so will make it pasty), then add just enough milk to make the mash thick, but not compact.

Drain the cooked meat over a saucepan, and reserve the broth. Discard the vegetables and shred the meat. Sauté remaining onion in oil over low heat, then add the meat and a ladleful of broth to keep the meat tender. Season with salt, pepper, and parsley and cook until all the broth has been absorbed. Meanwhile, over high heat, reduce the rest of the broth by half.

In a shallow baking dish, place a layer of mashed potato, then the meat, then cover with the remaining potato. Brown under the broiler or grill for a few minutes.

When you remove it from the oven, pour on the hot reduced broth. Traditionally, this masterpiece of popular cooking is served with a plain green salad. Accompany with a red Loire Valley wine.

TIAN D'AGNEAU AUX OLIVES

Provencal Lamb and Olive Tian (Jean-Jacques Raffiani, Paris Main d'Or)

A tian is a shallow, round earthenware dish traditionally used in Provence. Like terrine for example, the same word describes both the dish itself and the vessel in which it is cooked.

4 tablespoons olive oil
3 lb (1½ kg) boneless shoulder of lamb, cut into cubes about 2 oz (50 g) each
3 large onions, peeled and sliced
6 cloves garlic, peeled and crushed
4 large ripe tomatoes, peeled, seeded and roughly chopped (see page 33)
1 tablespoon tomato paste (concentrate)
1 green bell pepper (capsicum), cut into strips
1 bouquet garni comprising 3 sprigs parsley, 1 small stalk thyme, and 1 bay leaf
Salt

Ground pepper
6½ oz (200 g) green and black olives, pitted
1 chicken stock cube mixed with 250 ml (1 cup) water

In a large skillet, heat half the oil until it starts to smoke then sauté the meat. When it has browned evenly on all sides, remove with a slotted spoon to a shallow dish.

Lower the heat, add remaining oil to pan and soften the onions. Add the garlic, tomatoes, concentrate, bell pepper, bouquet garni, salt, and pepper. Mix well and simmer for 30 minutes until the sauce thickens, stirring from time to time.

Preheat oven to 360°F (180°C, gas mark 4). Remove sauce from heat. Stir in the olives, the meat, and all the juices from the dish. Pour into a tian or other baking dish, cover with stock and bake for 1½ hours.

Serve with potatoes boiled in salted water, and encourage each diner to mash the potato in the sauce with the back of his or her fork. For a dish as hardy and tasty as this, you can—just this once—forgo what would generally be considered "good" table manners. Accompany with a Mercurey.

TRAVERS DE PORCELET AU MIEL, PUREE A LA CIVE

Honey-glazed Suckling Pig Ribs with Herbed Mashed Potato
(Thierry Colas, Marty)

1½ lb (800 g) firm potatoes (such as
  charlottes or BF 15s), peeled and washed
⅓ cup (100 ml) dark soy sauce
⅓ cup (100 ml) acacia honey
1½ lb (800 g) rack of ribs from a suckling pig
½ cup (100 g) butter, at room temperature
⅓ cup (100 ml) milk, warm
1 small bunch sprouted shallots or scallions
  (spring onions)
1 chicken stock cube mixed with 250 ml
  (1 cup) water
Rock salt

Place potatoes in a saucepan, cover with cold water, salt, and bring to a boil. Cook 20 to 30 minutes, until the tip of a knife meets no resistance.

Meanwhile, preheat oven to 360°F (180°C, gas mark 4). Mix the soy sauce and honey in a bowl then brush the mixture onto the ribs in a roasting pan. Place the meat in the oven for 10 to 15 minutes, basting every 2 minutes with the remaining sauce. They should be glistening, shiny, and caramelized.

The potatoes should be done by this point. Drain, return to the saucepan with the butter, mash with the back of a fork, add enough milk to reach the desired consistency, neither too thick nor too runny. Keep warm in a double boiler.

Now it should be the ribs' turn to be ready. Place on a platter, switch off the oven and keep warm, using the residual heat to warm the dinner plates as well. Use warm stock to lift off the baked-on pan juices, and cook for 2 to 3 minutes to reduce, scraping gently with a spatula.

Chop the greens of the onions or shallots and mix into the potatoes. Slice between each rib, place the ribs on one side of the plate, the mash on the other, pour on the sauce and immediately serve this marvel of a dish, balanced between the Oriental and the Occidental, between invention and tradition.

Accompany with a bottle of red Graves.

CÔTE DE VEAU FOYOT, POMMES SAUTÉES

"Foyots" Veal Chops with Sautéed Potatoes (André Signoret, Le Train Bleu)

3 tablespoons butter
4 oz (125 g) white bread crumbs
4 oz (125 g) gruyère or other Swiss-type
  cheese, grated
4 prime veal chops, bone in, about 8 oz (250 g)
  each
2 lb (1 kg) firm potatoes (such as BF 15s),
  peeled, washed and cut in very thin slices,
  wiped with a cloth to remove starch
Salt
Freshly ground pepper
1 small bunch flat leaf parsley, washed, patted
  dry and stems removed
6 tablespoons peanut (groundnut) oil
$3\frac{1}{2}$ oz (100 g) all-purpose (plain) flour

Sauce

1 cup (250 ml) veal fond
1 small glass port
Scant 1 cup (190 g) butter

Several hours in advance or the night before, make the "Foyot" garnish by mixing together half the butter, the breadcrumbs, and grated cheese. Place the mixture on a plate, and form a round shape, about 4 in (10 cm) across and $1\frac{3}{4}$ in (4 cm) high, and reserve in the refrigerator.

In a large non-stick pan, melt 3 tablespoons of the butter and 4 tablespoons of the oil (or substitute $3\frac{1}{2}$ oz/100 g goose fat, delicious!) and sauté the potatoes over medium heat about 30 minutes, turning

very carefully from time to time, as they brown. When the potatoes are done, add salt, pepper, and the chopped parsley.

While the potaotes are cooking, start on the sauce, so that it will be ready at the same time. Boil the veal fond in a saucepan over medium heat until reduced by half. Reduce the port in a separate pan until it becomes syrupy, then add the fond and reduce to scant 1 cup (220 ml). Finally, whisk in the butter, bit by bit, to thicken.

When the potatoes are half done, light the broiler or grill. Season the veal chops, dust lightly with flour, shaking off any excess, and cook in a heavy ovenproof skillet, in the remaining butter and oil, about 7 minutes per side, over medium heat.

When you turn the meat over, place a $\frac{1}{2}$-in (1-cm) slice of the Foyot mixture on each chop. Finish cooking in the pan, then grill in the oven for 5 minutes until brown.

Place a chop on each plate, with sauce to one side, and the potatoes to the other, and savor this sparkling jewel of bourgeoise cuisine. A good Saint-Estèphe or other red Bordeaux would be a good choice of wine for accompanying this dish.

ROGNONS DE VEAU BEAUGE ET LEUR PUREE

Beaujolais-style Calves Kidneys with Mashed Potato
(Patrick Rayer, La Rôtisserie du Beaujolais)

2 lb (1 kg) firm potatoes (such as BF 15s)
$^2/_3$–1 cup (150–250 ml) milk
2 large calves' kidneys, fat removed, cut into
    cubes about $^3/_4$-in ($1^1/_2$-cm) square
1 tablespoon goose fat or peanut oil
1/2 cup (100 g) butter
Rock salt and table salt
Freshly ground pepper

Sauce

4 shallots, peeled and finely chopped
1 teaspoon butter
$^3/_4$ cup (200 ml) dry white wine (a Mâcon,
    if available)
$^3/_4$ cup (200 ml) veal fond
$^2/_3$ cup (150 ml) heavy (double) cream
1 heaped tablespoon Dijon mustard

Forty-five minutes before the meal, prepare old-fashioned mashed potatoes that will be the perfect foil for your kidneys. Peel and wash the potatoes, place in pan, cover with cold water and a little rock salt. Bring to a boil, cook 30 minutes, then drain, pass through a food mill into a mixing bowl containing ½cup (100 g) butter. Mix with a whisk, add just enough milk to reach the desired consistency, neither too stiff nor too liquidy. Keep warm over a double boiler.

Less than 30 minutes before sitting down to dinner, start the sauce. Sauté the shallots in butter over low heat then add the wine and reduce over high heat until there is only the equivalent of 2 teaspoons of juice left in the pan. Add the fond, and when it boils, add the cream. Cook over low heat stirring often, until the sauce coats the back of a spoon. Add the mustard and mix well.

Now take care of the kidneys. Season them, then heat the oil or fat in a non-stick pan and fry the kidneys over high heat no more than 5 minutes. Their centers should still be pink.

Drain, wipe the pan gently with paper towel, then add the sauce to deglaze the pan, gently removing the cooked on juice in the pan. Add the kidneys, stir quickly and serve at once with the mashed potatoes. Accompany with a Brouilly or a Régnié.

BLANQUETTE DE VEAU A LA VANILLE ET AUX AGRUMES

Veal Stew Scented with Vanilla and Citrus Fruit (Stéphane Baron, Le Zéphyr)

Prepare side vegetables of fresh spinach, steamed leek or basmati rice during the cold season, beans or peas in the spring or summer.

2 lb (1 kg) slighty fatty cuts of veal (breast, flank, rump) cubed, briefly blanched then rinsed under cold running water
1 carrot, peeled and finely chopped
1 leek, washed and finely chopped
1 onion, peeled and finely chopped
1 bouquet garni comprising 1 bay leaf, 1 sprig thyme, and 3 sprigs parsley
3 limes
1 plump vanilla bean
1 tablespoon butter
2 tablespoons all-purpose (plain) flour
2 pink grapefruits, carefully peeled, membrane removed, to garnish
20 g crème fraîche, or failing that heavy (double) cream
Rock salt, table salt, white peppercorns, freshly ground pepper
Side vegetables of your choice

Place onions, carrot, and leek in a pot with the bouquet garni, meat, 2 of the limes cut in half, the split vanilla bean, a sprinkling of rock salt, and a few peppercorns. Cover with cold water, bring to a boil, then simmer covered for 1½ hours.

Meanwhile, wash the remaining lime, and add its zest and juice to the crème fraîche; you will use it to finish the sauce.

When the stew is ready, remove the meat with a slotted spoon and place in a large saucepan. Strain the cooking bouillon through a chinois or sieve, scrape the vanilla seeds from the bean and discard the solids. Reserve 2 cups (500 ml) bouillon, pour the rest over the meat and hold over medium heat.

In another pan, melt the butter over low heat until it begins to sizzle, add the flour, stirring o ccasionally, for about 5 minutes, keeping the heat low so that it does not brown (this is called a white roux). Add the reserved 2 cups bouillon and continue to cook, stirring until the liquid thickens, like custard sauce. Correct the seasoning, remove from heat and add the lime-flavored cream. Stir well.

To assemble, plate the vegetables first, topped with drained meat, cover with the sauce and decorate with an odd number of grapefruit slices (which is much more attractive). Enjoy this dish with a glass of Pouilly Fumé.

POIRES ROTIES AU
CARAMEL DE FRUITS SECS

Roast Pears with Nut Caramel Sauce (Flora Mikula, Les Olivades)

4 pears (such as *doyenné-du-comice, beurré-* Hardy or other juicy pears), peeled
3 cinnamon sticks
1 vanilla bean, split lengthwise
6$\frac{1}{2}$ oz (200 g) acacia honey
Juice of 1 lemon
6$\frac{1}{2}$ oz (200 g) sugar
2 cups (500 ml) heavy (double) cream
8 oz (250 g) nuts (such as almonds, hazelnuts, walnuts, and pistachios)

Orange Flower Ice Cream
1 cup (250 ml) milk
1 cup (250 ml) heavy (double) cream
3$\frac{1}{2}$ oz (100 g) sugar
5 egg yolks
$\frac{1}{3}$ cup (100 ml) orange flower water

Start by making the orange flower ice cream. Heat the milk and the cream but remove from heat as soon as it comes to a boil. Beat the sugar and egg yolks until the mixture thickens and becomes pale. Gradually add the warm milk and cream, whisk thoroughly then pour the mixture back into the saucepan, heat over low heat, stirring constantly with a wooden spoon until thickened like custard. If the cream curdles, pour it into a blender or liquidizer and process until smooth. Remove from heat and cool. Mix the orange flower water into the cooled cream, and pour into your ice cream maker, following the manufacturer's instructions. If you do not have an ice cream maker, buy vanilla or cinnamon ice cream of excellent quality.

Preheat oven to 410°F (210°C, gas mark 6$\frac{1}{2}$). Place the pears in a deep baking pan with the cinnamon and the vanilla bean. Pour the honey and lemon juice over the pears, add boiling water to half the height of the baking dish and bake for 20 to 30 minutes. The pears should be cooked but firm. Turn off oven, leaving the pears inside.

Just before serving, pour the sugar into a large saucepan and add a little water. Over high heat, melt the sugar until you obtain a golden brown caramel.

While making the caramel, bring the cream to a boil. When the caramel is ready, add the hot cream, in small batches, stirring vigorously. Don't worry about the boiling witches' cauldron, it looks alarming but will soon die down. Add the nuts and cook 5 minutes at a simmer.

Drain the pears, place in soup plates, cover with nut sauce and serve this voluptuous dessert with the ice cream. Accompany with a glass of Muscat de Beaumes de Venise.

FINANCIER TIEDE AUX POIRES, CREME A LA CHICOREE

Warm Pear Financier Cakes with Chicory Custard (Christian Etchebest, Le Troquet)

4 cups (1 liter) water
1³⁄₄ cups (400 g) sugar
3 tender-fleshed pears (such as *doyenné-du-comice*, *beurré*-Hardy or Williams), peeled
²⁄₃ cup (135 g) butter
3 egg whites
¹⁄₂ cup (75 g) ground almonds
²⁄₃ cup (75 g) flour
1 tablespoon confectioners' (icing) sugar
³⁄₄ cup (200 ml) heavy (double) cream, refrigerated
1 tablespoon liquid chicory (substitute with strong coffee)

Place the cream, the bowl and beaters for whipping the cream in the refrigerator.

In a saucepan, bring 1 liter of water to a boil with scant 1 cup (200 g) of the sugar. Drop the pears into the boiling syrup. Simmer 15 minutes, then leave to cool in the syrup.

Half an hour before mealtime, give your attention to the financiers, which will be served warm. Preheat the oven to 400°F (200°C, gas mark 6). Butter a non-stick baking sheet with ¹⁄₂ tablespoon butter. Melt the rest of the butter over very low heat. In a bowl, lightly whip the egg whites with a hand whisk, add ³⁄₄cup (180 g) of the sugar, ground almonds, flour, and finally the melted butter. Place four 3-in (8-cm) baking rings on the baking sheet and fill with the batter. If you don't have any baking rings, substitute with 4 small round non-stick pans, no larger than 4-in (10-cm) in diameter.

Drain the pears. Cut each one into 8 wedges, remove the core, and arrange 6 slices in a flower on top of each financier. Place into the oven for 12 minutes and, 2 minutes before they are done, sprinkle with confectioners' (icing) sugar, which will make the cakes exquisitely golden. Remove the circles or unmold, and place in the center of a dessert plate, pear side up.

At the last minute, whip the cream (see page 37), add the remaining 2 teaspoons sugar half way through and the chicory, place a large dollop (use a soup spoon rinsed under hot water) on each cake. Serve immediately with a glass of sweet Jurançon.

PAIN PERDU AUX POMMES

Apple Bread Puddding (Philippe Tredgeu, Chez Casimir)

3 eggs
1 cup (250 ml) milk
³/₄ cup (175 g) sugar
Seeds of 1 vanilla bean (see Helpful hint)
4 thick slices sourdough bread, stale or fresh
2 large apples, juicy and flavorful (such as el-
    stars or goldens)
¹/₂ cup (100 g) unsalted butter
2 tablespoons crème fraîche

In a bowl whisk together eggs, milk, ¹/₃ cup (75 g) of the sugar, and the vanilla seeds. Place the slices of bread in one layer, in a shallow dish into which they fit snugly then cover with the liquid. Leave the bread to soak for about 2 hours.

One hour before mealtime, preheat oven to 300°F (150°C, gas mark 2). Wash, dry, and cut the apples into 8 slices, remove the core but not the skin and place the 16 wedges in a baking dish that can also be heated over a flame. Pour the rest of the sugar into a small saucepan, and wet with a few spoonfuls of water. Cook over high heat, until it forms a golden caramel. Pour the boiling caramel over the apples then bake for 20 minutes. Turn the slices over three times, very carefully, so as not to break them. Watch them closely. They should look candied but not burnt. Add a little water during cooking, if needed. Remove the dish from the oven and leave to cool to room temperature.

When you are ready to serve the dessert, heat the butter over medium heat until it sizzles (the French say it "sings"). Pick up the slices of bread with a slotted spatula, drain slightly, and cook 3 to 4 minutes on each side, until golden.

Place the bread in the center of the dessert plates and discard any remaining butter. Arrange the apple slices on the bread. Place the baking dish over high heat, add the cream and scrape gently with a wooden spoon to detach all the baked on juices. Stir well and pour a little sauce around each pudding.

Enjoy this marvelous dessert immediately. It has satisfied the poor since time immemorial, even if it is usually served, as you can well imagine, in a much simpler form. Accompany with a glass of Côteaux-du-Layon.

Helpful hints: Remove the seeds of the vanilla bean by splitting it lengthways and scraping out the seeds with the side of a knife. Keep the husk of the bean in a jar of sugar to flavor it, if desired. Accompany with a glass of Côteaux-du-Layon.

CHAUD-FROID DE FRUITS ROUGES PARFUME

Summer Fruit Gratin (Stéphane Baron, Le Zéphyr)

4 egg yolks

Scant $\frac{1}{2}$ cup (100 g) sugar

4 tablespoons sweet white wine (substitute with water)

Your choice of flavoring: a pinch of dried lavander flowers, or a few drops of lavender extract; or 1 teaspoon rose flower water or berry flavored spirits; or the seeds from a vanilla bean

2 cups (500 ml) heavy (double) cream, refrigerated

$\frac{1}{2}$ cup (50 g) + 1 tablespoon confectioners' (icing) sugar

1 kg (500 g) summer berries, preferably 8 oz (250 g) strawberries, 4 oz (125 g) raspberries, blackberries or blueberries, and 4 oz (125 g) red or black currants

An hour before sitting down to dinner, make the sabayon. You have no idea how easy it is! Place the cream, the bowl and beaters for the whipped cream in the refrigerator. Partially fill the sink with cold water and ice cubes. In the non-reactive top of a double-boiler over simmering water, beat the yolks, sugar, and wine (or water) with a whisk or electric beaters. The result will be a pale mousse, airy and compact at the same time. Remove from the heat as soon as it has thickened, move to the sink and continue beating until completely cooled. Add the flavor of your choice. Whip the cream (see page 37), adding the confectioners' sugar when it starts to form peaks. Gently fold it into the sabayon and reserve in the refrigerator.

Wash and dry the berries then arrange in four ovenproof soup plates or other shallow individual baking dishes. Just before serving, light the broiler (grill). Pour the sabayon over the berries, sprinkle with the remaining 1 tablespoon confectioners' sugar, then place in oven just a few instants to brown. Serve immediately.

This dessert is even tastier with an acidic sorbet, like apricot or lemon, which will provide a fine contrast of flavor. Accompany with a glass of Gewurztraminer or a late harvest Riesling.

SOUPE DE FRAISES/
GLACE AUX HERBES

Strawberry Soup with Herb Ice Cream
(Catherine Guerraz, Chez Catherine)

This dessert is best prepared the night before, or the morning of the dinner. Serves 6

**2 cups (500 ml) red wine, preferably a
  Bordeaux**
³/₄ cup (160 g) sugar
6 green peppercorns
1 tea bag
2 lb (1 kg) strawberries, washed and stemmed

Ice cream
¹/₂ cup (250 ml) milk
¹/₂ cup (250 ml) heavy (double) cream
**8 egg yolks (use the whites to make a panna
  cotta on page 132)**
Scant ¹/₂ cup (100 g) sugar
**8 sprigs of basil, chervil, and dill, washed and
  patted dry**

Start with the ice cream. Reserve a few herb leaves to garnish then place the rest in the freezer for 20 minutes before chopping finely. Heat the milk and the cream in a saucepan. As soon as the mixture begins to boil, remove from heat. In a mixing bowl, beat yolks and sugar until they become pale and thick. Gradually add the slightly cooled creamy milk, stirring constantly with a wooden spoon. Return to saucepan over low heat, still stirring, and cook until thick enough to coat the back of the spoon (don't worry if the mixture curdles). Process in a blender or liquidizer until smooth. Remove from heat, add the herbs, and leave to cool. Then pour into an ice cream maker, and follow the manufacturer's instructions. If you do not have an ie cream maker, buy a good vanilla ice cream. In either case, remember to move the ice cream from the freezer to the refrigerator when sitting down to dinner, so that it will reach the ideal consistency by serving time.

Nothing could be simpler than the soup, but it does require a little bit of time. Heat the wine with the sugar, pepper, and tea bag. Simmer until reduced and slightly syrupy, about 30 minutes.

Add the strawberries to the syrup and simmer for 3 minutes. Discard the tea bag, pour the soup into a bowl and leave to cool, then chill in the refrigerator until serving. When ready, serve the soup in soup plates, top with a scoop of ice cream (shaped with a spoon dipped in hot water). Decorate this very old-fashioned dessert with the reserved herbs. A chilled muscat along side would be nothing less than enchanting.

the fruits, remove the stems but not the pits (stones) from the cherries, or they will lose their juice, and their flavor, during cooking. For the apricots, split them in half and discard the pit. Place the fruit in the buttered dish, stir the batter that had been resting, pour over the fruit and bake for 45 minutes. Half way through, cut the remaining butter into small pieces and place evenly over the top, then sprinkle with the fine sugar. This will make it even more golden, crisp and appetizing. Enjoy this traditional cake, still warm from the oven. You will never tire of it, served with a glass of chilled dry white wine.

CLAFOUTIS AUX FRUITS D'ETE

Summer Fruit Clafoutis (André Signoret, Le Train Bleu)

Scant ¹/₂ cup (50 g) flour
¹/₄ cup (60 g) granulated sugar and 1 table-
spoon superfine (caster) sugar
3 eggs
1 tablespoon olive oil
2 cups (500 ml) whole milk
1 small glass kirsch
¹/₃ cup (60 g) butter
1 lb (500 g) very ripe fruit (such as apricots
from the Roussillon or plump black cherries)

Make the batter 1 hour before cooking as it needs time to rest. In a mixing bowl, mix flour and granulated sugar then, using a wooden spoon, very thoroughly mix in the eggs, oil, and milk in thirds, and the kirsch. Set aside (at kitchen room temperature).

One hour later, butter a 2-in (5-cm) high earthenware dish with half the butter and preheat the oven to 360°F (180°C, gas mark 4). Wash and dry

MELI-MELO D'AGRUMES

Citrus Tutti Frutti
(Benoît Chagny, Λ & M Le Bistrot)

5 oranges
Seeds of 2 vanilla beans (see page 126)
A few thyme buds
A few sprigs of mint
3 pink grapefruit

Extract the juice of 1 orange. Wash the other 4 and remove all of their zest with a zester. Mix the zests, juice, vanilla seeds, thyme, and a few finely chopped mint leaves.

With a sharp paring knife, remove the peel and membrane from the oranges and grapefruit, carefully separating into sections. Add the extra juices to the seasoned mixture. Arrange the fruit attractively in shallow bowls, cover with juice and serve very well chilled, after leaving it to marinate in the refrigerator.

If you have some vanilla ice cream, a small scoop on top of each bowl would be very pretty, topped with half a vanilla bean and garnished with a little mint. Almond tuiles (see page 130) and a Corsican muscat will bring you to perfection.

MINESTRONE DE FRUITS EXOTIQUES AU GINGEMBRE

Tropical Fruit Minestrone with Ginger
(Patrice Contrand, Marty)

Prepare this dessert the night before or in the morning for an evening meal.

1 small piece fresh ginger, peeled and grated
2/3 cup (150 g) sugar
2 cups (500 ml) water
1 small Victoria (or other) pineapple (leaves on top should detach easily when ripe), peeled and cut into small cubes
2 very ripe kiwis, peeled and cut into small cubes
1 very ripe but firm mango, peeled and cut into small cubes

Citrus sorbet
Juice of 1 large yellow grapefruit
Juice of 2 large oranges
Juice of 3 or 4 plump lemons
Scant $^1/_2$ cup (100 g) sugar
$^1/_3$ cup (100 ml) water

Start by making the citrus sorbet. Bring the juices, sugar, and water to a boil. Cool, and place in an ice cream maker, following the manufacturers' instructions. If you do not have an ice cream maker, buy an orange, grapefruit, or lemon sorbet. Place the ginger in a saucepan. Add the sugar and water, bring to a rolling boil, remove from heat and infuse 10 minutes, then strain and chill the syrup. Combine cubed fruit and syrup and marinate in the refrigerator. Serve in shallow dishes with a scoop of ice cream in the middle of the "minestrone." The taste and lightness are perfect. A late harvest Gewurztraminer will only add to your pleasure.

TARTE FINE CHAUDE AUX POMMES

Hot Apple Tartlets (André Cellier, Brasserie Mollard)

4 plump reinette apples, peeled, quartered
  and cored, each quarter cut in two (to yield
  32 chunks)
$^2/_3$ cup (150 g) sugar
1 package best quality puff pastry, about
  8–10 oz (250–300 g)
4 golden apples
$^1/_4$ cup (50 g) butter

Place the 32 reinette apple chunks in a saucepan with scant $^1/_2$ cup (100 g) of the sugar and a little water. Cook the apples until they form a thick apple sauce, mashing any large lumps with the back of a fork.

An hour or so before serving the dessert, preheat the oven to 400°F (200°C, gas mark 6). Roll out the pastry as thinly as possible on a dry, clean work surface. Using a dessert plate as a guide, cut out 4 bases with a sharp paring knife. Cover a baking sheet with baking parchment, place the pastry bases on it, cover each one with a thin layer of apple sauce. Peel the goldens and cut each in half. Flat side down, cut each half into very thin slices and arrange them in a flower pattern on each tart. Spinkle with the rest of the sugar and the butter. Bake for about 20 minutes, until the tops and the pastry are golden. Serve this marvelous classic hot, accompanied by a sweet wine. With a scoop of vanilla ice cream, it becomes a tart à la mode but, to some, doing so makes it too rich.

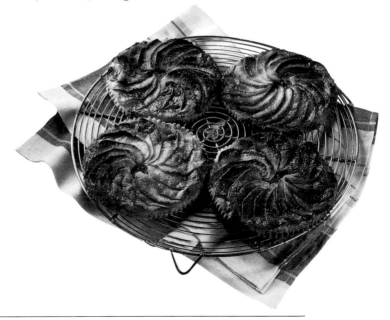

LATTE COTTO ET SES TUILES AUX AMANDES

Panna Cotta and Almond Wafers (Philippe Tredgeu, Chez Casimir)

1$\frac{1}{2}$ cups (375 ml) whole milk
$\frac{1}{2}$ cup (125 g) heavy (double) cream
Scant $\frac{1}{2}$ cup (100 g) sugar
Grated zest of 2 lemons or limes
Seeds of 1 vanilla bean (see Helpful hint,
    page 126)
5 egg whites, lightly whisked

Wafers

Grated zest and juice of 1 orange
$\frac{1}{3}$ cup (75 g) butter, melted
$\frac{1}{2}$ cup (50 g) flour, sifted
$\frac{1}{2}$ cup (75 g) blanched almonds, chopped
Scant 2/3 cup (125 g) sugar

A few hours before mealtime, make the batter for the tuiles (wafers). In a mixing bowl, combine the orange zest and juice, butter, flour, almonds, and sugar. Mix thoroughly then reserve in the refrigerator to firm up somewhat.

Preheat oven to 250°F (120°C, gas mark $\frac{1}{2}$).

In a saucepan, with a wooden spoon, mix together milk, cream, sugar, lemon or lime zests, and vanilla seeds. Bring to a boil, then remove from heat and cool for 15 minutes. Pour the mixture through a sieve or chinois, onto the whisked egg. Mix well, strain again, and pour into 4 shallow ceramic or earthenware ramekins or ovenproof soup plates that hold about 1 cup (250 ml) liquid. Bake for 30 to 45 mintues. They should be set, but the cream should still jiggle when shaken gently. Cool to room temperature.

Just before sitting down to dinner, make the tuiles. (They can actually be made up to two days in advance, but are infinitely better fresh.) Preheat the oven to 500°F (250°C, gas mark 10). If you do not have a non-stick baking sheet, wipe yours with a little oil on a paper towel. Drop 1 teaspoonful of batter on sheet, flatten slightly with the back of the spoon, and continue, leaving space between to allow for spreading. Slip tray into the oven for 4 to 5 minutes until the tuiles are golden.

Remove and allow to cool 1 minute, lift each tuile with a spatula and quickly place it on any cylindrical object at hand (bottle, rolling pin) to form a curved shape. The contrast of creaminess and crispiness is nothing but suave. Try accompanying this dessert with a glass of Champagne.

POTS VANILLE ET CHOCOLAT, MADELEINES A L'ANIS

Vanilla and Chocolate Creams with Anise Madeleines
(Christian Etchebest, Le Troquet)

Vanilla and Chocolate Creams

> **4 cups (1 liter) whole milk**
> **2 whole eggs, plus 8 yolks (10 eggs total)**
> **Scant 1 cup (200 g) sugar**
> **1 vanilla bean from Tahiti, or 2 standard "bourbon" vanilla beans**
> **$^1\!/_4$ cup (25 g) unsweetened cocoa powder**

Madeleines (small French cakes)

> **2 eggs**
> **Scant $^2\!/_3$ cup (125 g) sugar**
> **$^1\!/_3$ cup (100 ml) milk**
> **$1^2\!/_3$ cups (200 g) flour**
> **1 level teaspoon baking powder**
> **$^1\!/_2$ cup (100 g) butter, melted + $^1\!/_2$ tablespoon butter at room temperature**
> **$^1\!/_2$ teaspoon ground aniseseed**
> **2 tablespoons confectioners' (icing) sugar, if desired**

Make the creams in advance, so that they will have time to cool. Bring half the milk to a boil, with the split vanilla bean(s), remove from heat and set aside to infuse. Meanwhile beat 1 whole egg, 4 egg yolks, and half the sugar, until it starts to whiten. Scrape out the seeds from the beans, add to the milk, discard the bean, then gradually pour milk into the eggs, stirring constantly with a wooden spoon. Strain mixture through a sieve or chinois and fill 6 ovenproof clay pots or 6 ramekins. Repeat exactly the same process with the remaining ingredients, replacing the vanilla with the cocoa powder.

Heat the oven to 200°F (100°C, gas mark $^1\!/_2$), or as close as you can get. Place the pots in a baking pan, pour hot water around them, and bake for 45 minutes to 1 hour. The water should not boil. If it does, add a little cold water. The cream should set, but still be soft enough to tremble when lightly shaken. To check, insert a knife; the blade should come out wet, but clean. Cool to room temperature.

Make the madeleines just before the meal, as they're at their best when they are still warm. Preheat the oven to 425°F (220°C, gas mark 7). In a mixing bowl, whisk together the eggs and the sugar, then add the milk, then the flour and baking powder sifted together, the melted butter, and the aniseseed. With the remaining butter, grease 2 non-stick madeleine pans (scalloped-shaped pans). Fill the molds (preferably small) and bake for 7 to 8 minutes. They should rise and be golden. Unmold while still warm onto a wire rack.

To serve, place one vanilla and one chocolate cream on each plate, along with three or four madeleines, sprinkled with confectioners' sugar if desired. Accompany with a Jurançon doux.

FONDANT AU CHOCOLAT,
SAUCE AU CARAMEL DEMI-SEL

Chocolate Fudge Cake with Salt Toffee Sauce (Catherine Guerraz, Chez Catherine)

4 squares (4 oz/120 g) dark chocolate (minimum 55% cocoa)

$^3/_4$ cup (150 g) butter (use $^1/_2$ tablespoon of this to grease the dishes)

4 eggs

$^2/_3$ cup (150 g) sugar

$^1/_2$ cup (60 g) flour, sifted

Salt toffee sauce

$^2/_3$ cup (150 g) sugar

Juice of half a lemon

$^1/_4$ cup (50 g) salted butter

$^1/_3$ cup (100 g) heavy (double) cream

Melt the chocolate and butter in the top of a double boiler. Meanwhile, beat together the eggs and sugar until it begins to rise and become pale. Add the flour, then the melted butter and chocolate, mixing well after each addition. Butter 6 individual soufflé dishes, about 3-in (8-cm) across and 2$^1/_2$-in (6-cm) high, and fill to within $^1/_2$-in (1-cm) from the top. If you do not have individual molds, a small casserole dish will suffice. Chill to set slightly.

Use this time to make the Salt Toffee Sauce. In a saucepan, cook the sugar with a small quantity of water, and make a golden caramel. Add the lemon juice, stir thoroughly, add the butter, stir again until it is melted, then add the cream, still stirring constantly. Pour this amber liquid into a bowl, cool to room temperature then reserve in the refrigerator.

Half an hour before serving, finish the cakes. Preheat the oven to 400°F (200°C, gas mark 6). Bake 12 minutes for the small molds, 20 minutes for a larger dish. The top should be solid. Leave to rest a few minutes, then unmold onto plates, and draw a ring of sauce around them.

This rich, incredibly suave dessert, would be a regal ending to a light meal. Try serving a Rivesaltes or vintage port.

GATEAU DE RIZ, CREME ANGLAISE

Rice Pudding with Custard (Patrick Rayer, La Rôtisserie du Beaujolais)

Make this cake several days before serving and only prepare the custard on the day of the meal iteslf.

$^3/_4$ **cup (150 g) short grain rice, preferably Arborio**
3 cups (750 ml) whole milk
1 vanilla bean, split
Sacnt 1$^1/_2$ cups (300 g) sugar
5 oz (150 g) candied fruit (or mixed peel), diced small, or golden raisins (sultanas), soaked in cold water
Pinch table salt

Custard

1 cup (250 ml) whole milk
1 vanilla bean, split
4 egg yolks
5 teaspoons sugar

Boil the rice for 3 minutes in a large quantity of water. Drain. Bring the milk to a boil with the salt and the split vanilla bean, then add the rice and cook, barely simmering, until the milk has completely evaporated, about 45 minutes. Stir gently from time to time, to prevent the rice from sticking.

Put half the sugar in a saucepan, moisten with a little water, and cook without stirring to make a dark caramel. Pour it immediately into a 8-in (20-cm) non-stick loaf pan, and quickly but carefully tilt in all directions to coat the sides. Preheat oven to 360°F (180°C, gas mark 4).

Carefully mix the rice, the remaining sugar, and the fruit and pour into the pan. Place in a baking tray, filled with boiling water and bake for approximately 30 minutes, until the top browns. Cool, then store in refrigerator.

The day the dish is to be served, make the Custard Sauce. Heat the milk with the split vanilla bean, remove from heat as soon as it boils, let infuse and cool slightly. Beat the yolks and the sugar until they become thick and pale. Scrape out the vailla beans, add to the milk, discard bean. Very gradually, stir the milk into the eggs, return mixture to the saucepan and heat over low heat, stirring with a wooden spoon, until it becomes thick enough to coat the back of the spoon. Remove from heat, pour into bowl and cool. If you cook it too long and it curdles, process in a blender or liquidizer until smooth and thick.

To serve, briefly dip the pan into boiling water, unmold and cut the pudding into thin slices. Each diner will pour his or her own custard while emitting loud sighs of contentment. Accompany with a Jurançon moëlleux.

CREPES SUZETTE AU GRAND MARNIER

Crepes Suzette with Grand Marnier (André Cellier, Brasserie Mollard)

Scant 2 cups (200 g) flour, sifted
5 teaspoons sugar
Large pinch salt
2 eggs
2 cups (500 ml) whole milk
1 tablespoon peanut oil or melted butter, plus
    a little extra for the pan
1 tablespoon Grand Marnier (or failing that,
    rum)

Sauce
  $\frac{1}{2}$ cup (100 g) butter
  Scant $\frac{1}{2}$ cup (100 g) sugar
  1 orange and 1 lemon
  4 tablespoons Grand Marnier

Make the batter the night before cooking, or the morning of the dinner, as it needs to rest for several hours in the refrigerator before being used. In a bowl, mix the flour, sugar, and salt. Whisk in the eggs, then the milk, oil (or butter), and finally the spirits. Cover and chill.

A few minutes before mealtime, rouse the batter with a little whisking, and make the crêpes (pancakes). Using a paper towel, grease a 10-in (25-cm) crêpe pan with a little oil. Place the pan over high heat, and when hot, pour a small ladleful of batter, tilt the pan to coat completely, cook the first side until golden then turn it over with a spatula (if you are a beginner) or by flipping it into the air with a flick of the wrist (if you have had practice). You should make about 10 crêpes. Reserve, stacked on a plate.

When ready to serve, fold the crêpes into quarters. In a frying pan of chafing dish, make the sauce. Melt the butter and sugar and cook over moderate heat until a golden caramel forms. While they are cooking, wash and dry the orange and lemon, remove their zest and extract the juice of the whole orange but only half the lemon.

When the caramel is ready, stop the cooking process by adding the lemon juice, then add the zests, stirring briefly.

Pour in orange juice and stir again, place the crêpes in the sauce so they absorb liquid while reheating. When the sauce becomes a thick syrup, pour in the Grand Marinier and carefully set alight to flambé, while gently shaking the pan, so that the burning alcohol covers the crêpes uniformly. Place two crêpes on each plate, top with a little syrup and serve this great classic as it is presented in Parisian brasseries where traditions live on, piping hot. Accompany with a glass of Champagne.

ACKNOWLEDGMENTS

The recipes selected for this book are not only easy to prepare and their ingredients readily available, but they all hold considerable cultural value. The chefs themselves are both staunch defenders of their know-how and innovators, a dual passion without which there is no true quality.

The chefs

Stéphane Baron: Born in Paris to parents who moved from Brittany and Charentes, this young chef has turned the beautiful Ménilmontant restaurant where he labors into an establishment whose reputation extends beyond the confines of his neighborhood. He gives pride of place to seafood and adores spices and heady flavors.
Le Zéphyr, 1 rue du Jourdain, 75020

Benoît Chagny: Born in Normandy, he was given responsibility by Jean-Pierre Vigato, the owner of Apicius, and François Grandjean, owner of Marius (two of the capital's acclaimed restaurants), for one of their two bistros. Short cooking times, technical perfection and elegant simplicity have made the reputation of both the bistro and this young chef.
A & M Le Bistrot, 105 rue de Prony, 75017

Thierry Colas: This young chef from Normandy has taken over one of the most beautiful 1930s brasseries in the capital, serving high-precision cuisine, where brasserie classics rub shoulders with highly inventive dishes. The desserts of pastry chef Patrice Contrand, born in Paris to parents originally from the Périgord and Normandy, are marvels of subtlety.
Marty, 20 avenue des Gobelins, 75005

Christian Etchebest: Born in the Basque Country, with his coarse yet sunny accent, this young chef loves his region of origin and displays a most infectious enthusiasm. His demanding cuisine is an example of tradition exalted by audacity, and imagination that transforms his skill into sheer poetry.
Le Troquet, 21 rue François Bonvin, 75015

Tsukasa Fukuyama: This young Japanese chef works at the annex of Apicius and Marius in the 16th arrondissement. To the clear, precise, and elegant style of the establishment he brings his attention to detail and his perfectionism.
A & M Le Bistrot, 136 boulevard Murat, 75016

Catherine Guerraz: Born in Aquitaine to parents who owned a restaurant in Nice, this young, self-taught cook was brought up in the shadow of the stove. People throng to sample her market dishes, full of freshness and sensuality, just like their chef.
Chez Catherine, 65 rue de Provence, 75009

Flora Mikula: Born in Nîmes to Polish parents who emigrated to Lorraine, and brought up by her

grandmother in Avignon where she attended hotel school, this young lover of Provence cooks up a cuisine that is a fine example of the balance between regional products and modern lightness.
Les Olivades, 41 avenue de Ségur, 75007

Jean-Jacques Raffiani: he watches with gruff amiability over his bistro, which is a gathering point for natives and aficionados of his island, serving a rustic cuisine, just like grandma made it, with all the honesty of an old craftsman and the scents of the wilds of Corsica.
Paris Main d'Or, 133 rue du Faubourg-Saint-Antoine, 75011

Patrick Rayer: this Burgundian, a member of the Académie Culinaire de France (which brings together the upper crust of French professional chefs), showers warmth and authority over the bistro of the most prestigious restaurant in Paris, La Tour d'Argent. He dedicates himself with talent to the cuisine and wines of the region between Lyon and Mâcon.
Rôtisserie du Beaujolais, 19 quai de la Tournelle, 75005

Joël Renty: Also a Burgundian and member of the Académie Culinaire de France, he is responsible for the cuisine of the historic monument that is the most beautiful Art Nouveau brasserie in Paris, the work of the architect Edouard Niermans. The traditional desserts are overseen by the pastry chef André Cellier, originally from Auvergne.
Mollard, 115 rue Saint-Lazare, 75008

André Signoret: From Bresse, rewarded by the Académie Culinaire de France, he manages the kitchen of the most extraordinary brasserie in Paris (according to Louise de Vilmorin). Listed as a historic monument, it bears startling testimony to the Belle Epoque style. There you can sample dishes in the greatest bourgeois tradition, discreetly lightened and modernized.
Le Train Bleu, Gare de Lyon, 20 boulevard Diderot, 75012

Philippe Tredgeu: In the shadow of the Church of Saint-Vincent-de-Paul this young chef from the Béarn serves up a cuisine that is freely inspired by his home region. His excellent bistro is frequently besieged, as is always the case in Paris when a fine restaurant opens and is lauded by gourmands who are the best form of advertisement a chef could hope for.
Chez Casimir, 6 rue de Belzunce, 75010

The author

Author Marie-Noël Rio has worked as a film editor, theatre director, and playwright and author of libretti and books on contemporary opera. Her rather unusual career has given her an original voice that has made her a success in food writing. One of her books, *Je Ne Sais Pas Recevoir* (I Can't Throw a Dinner Party), has been published in France, while another, *Je Ne Sais Pas Cuisiner* (I Can't Cook), has been published in France and Germany.

PERIPLUS WORLD COOKBOOKS

TRAVEL THE WORLD IN YOUR KITCHEN!

Welcome to the world's best-selling international cookery series—and the first comprehensive encyclopaedia of world cooking! Each volume contains over 70 easy-to-follow recipes gathered in the country of origin. Introductory essays by noted food writers explore the cuisine's cultural roots and all food photographs are taken on location to ensure absolute authenticity. Truly the ultimate cookbooks for globetrotting gourmets!

"The scope of this library of books transcends the size of its volumes...They are thoughtful, well-planned, well-edited, and most importantly they strive mightily for authenticity, an effort sadly lacking in so many of today's 'ethnic' cookery books."

– "A Gourmet At Large" *Gourmet Magazine*, USA

The Food of Australia
ISBN 962 593 393 X Hardcover

The Food of Bali
ISBN 962 593 385 9 Hardcover

The Food of Jamaica
ISBN 962 593 228 3 Hardcover

The Food of Japan
ISBN 962 593 392 1 Hardcover

The Food of North Italy
ISBN 962 593 505 3 Hardcover

The Food of Paris
ISBN 962 593 991 1 Hardcover

The Food of Sante Fe
ISBN 962 593 229 1 Hardcover

The Food of Texas
ISBN 962 593 534 7 Hardcover